The Disciples' Prayer

Ifeanyi Chris Agagbor

Copyright © 2007, 2008 by Ifeanyi Chris Agagbor

The Disciples' Prayer
by Ifeanyi Chris Agagbor

Printed in the United States of America

ISBN 978-1-60477-312-5

All rights reserved solely by the author. The author guarantees all contents are original and do not infringe upon the legal rights of any other person or work. No part of this book may be reproduced in any form without the permission of the author. The views expressed in this book are not necessarily those of the publisher.

Unless otherwise indicated, Bible quotations are taken from:

The New International Version. Copyright © 1973, 1978, 1984 by The Bible Societies and The New King James Version. Copyright © 1997 by Word Publishing.

www.xulonpress.com

Author's Autobiography

Ifeanyi Chris Agagbor (first time author) is a Nigerian-born U.S. citizen, born to late Chief Chukwudebe Richard Ogagbor (1928-2005) and late Mrs. Ifechukwude Patricia Ogagbor (nee Okondor; 1937-1981) on August 26 1959. He was educated in Nigeria where he obtained a B.Sc. degree in Human Nutrition (1986) from the University of Ibadan and a M.Sc. degree in Biochemistry (1990) from the University of Benin. From 1990-1999 he was a Lecturer in Biochemistry Department of a State-owned University. He relocated to the U.S. in 1999 through the DV-99 Immigrant Visa program. He is blessed with two sons; Oluchi (born 1995) and Fumnanya (born 2004). He has been a studious Bible student for over fifteen years, has a burning passion for the uncorrupted Word of GOD, and is a Monotheist (or Unitarian) Sabbatarian. He currently lives in Riverdale, MD.

Introduction

I have believed for quite sometime that the Disciples' Prayer (Mat. 6:9-13) which our Lord Yehshua the Messiah (Jesus Christ) gave us is a basic but efficacious prayer for all times. It is the Disciples' Prayer because it is the prayer format the Messiah gave to us; the Lord's Prayer is actually recorded in John 17. I initially started this project for personal and family use and it gradually evolved into what you are now reading; to GOD be the glory. I believe that what we say when communicating with the LORD in prayers is of utmost importance. If we take time to prepare speeches to address earthly dignitaries and gatherings, how much more are we expected to be mindful of what we say before the most awesome and majestic dignitary in all of creation?

This work is an exegesis (critical biblical explanation or interpretation) on the prayer our Lord Yehshua (Jesus) gave to us; it is a prayer of complete nakedness (unpretentious sincerity) before our awesome GOD and it is praying in the Word. Much more importantly, the prayer goes further to put the Word in the minds of Petitioners. The truth has been powerfully preached in several departments of our new life in Yehshua (Jesus), but it appears that in the area of prayer, our attitude implies that GOD will prefer our self-contrived ways of praying instead of the way HE has revealed to us in

HIS Word. Author is convinced that one of the reasons why most Believers do not pay much attention to this prayer is because of inadequate education with respect to the prayer points. Consequently, this aspect is dealt with in this book in prayer format. It cannot be over-stressed that answered prayers are not indicative of our good standing in the sight of GOD because even workers of iniquity have their prayers answered (Mt. 7:21-23). Without claiming that this is the only prayer that GOD acknowledges, the Author believes that this is the foundational life-transforming prayer and that all other prayers though supplementary are also important.

There are about 7 prayer points in the Believer's Prayer and can be summarized as noted below:

1. <u>Our Father in Heaven</u>: A brief invocation of GOD by outlining HIS main defining attributes (personal name, titles, nature and dwelling place).
2. <u>Hallowed Be Thy Name</u>: Praise GOD because of HIS awesome attributes such as creator of all the universe, holiness, righteousness and justice, love and compassion, faithfulness and mercy, self-revelation and foreknowledge, etc.
3. <u>Thy Kingdom come, Thy will be done on earth as is done in Heaven</u>: This kingdom prayer focuses on the reality of HIS kingdom, the power of HIS Word and the work of (the) holy spirit. It reminds us that GOD has made available everything necessary for our living a life of holiness through faith in Yehshua (Jesus).
4. <u>Give us the day our daily bread</u>: The providence prayer petitions GOD for our material needs. The Author humbly submits that most Christians are more than competent to tutor him in this section because it is based on diverse individual needs. Hence, this

The Disciples' Prayer

section has been severely condensed so as to be adaptable to Petitioners' peculiar needs.
5. <u>Forgive us our trespasses as we forgive those who offend us</u>: The forgiveness prayer deals with the vertical and horizontal components of the covenant of forgiveness which GOD makes with the repentant world through Yehshua (Jesus), HIS only begotten Son and our Lord and Savior.
6. <u>Lead us not into temptation</u>: The protection prayer solicits for GOD's help in preventing us from yielding (or succumbing) to sin or temptation; it is the spiritual warfare section and emphasizes the use of the weapons which GOD has made available to us for our victory.
7. <u>Deliver us from evil</u>: The deliverance prayer focuses on our need to be rescued from the grip of the evil that dwells in our flesh; this prayer point emphasizes the need to be delivered from ourselves.

It is not the Author's intention that this prayer be used as a recital. It is only meant to constantly keep before us the scriptural meanings of the Prayer Points Yehshua (Jesus) gave to us. Users are encouraged to make this prayer adaptable to their unique circumstances without tampering with the fundamental intent of our Lord. Another crucial advantage this prayer has is that it is packed with scriptural passages for the Users' verification. The prayer can therefore be used to enhance our bible study since some of its contents are highly controversial.

It is my sincere and humble hope that the LORD will continue to glorify and magnify HIS awesome and majestic name through this prayer given to us by HIS only begotten Son. Amen.

Our Father, in Heaven

Our heavenly FATHER, the LORD GOD almighty, the self-existing sovereign Spirit, the GOD of Abraham, Isaac and Jacob, the GOD of King David, the GOD of Yehshua (Jesus) and our Apostolic Fathers, we humbly come before YOU in prayers to renew our affirmation of our total dependence on YOU, our complete submission (or surrender) to YOUR authority and our firm commitment to be conformed to YOUR revealed righteous standards and principles. Amen. We surrender to YOU all that we are and all that YOU have given us to be used in the advancement of YOUR cause and for the greater glory of YOUR most holy name. Amen. We confidently approach YOUR throne of grace with the faith YOU have given us in Yehshua (Jesus) as our offering to YOU and pray that YOU perfectize this faith. Amen (Exo. 3:6; Mat. 22:33; Acts 7:32; Psa. 110:1; Joh. 20:17; 1 Pet. 1:3; Eph. 5:2; Rom. 15:16).

YOU O LORD are the only true GOD; before YOU, there was no GOD, nor will there be any after YOU; from eternity past, YOU have always been the GOD and will continue to be GOD forever and ever. Amen. YOU are the first and the last; apart from YOU there is no other GOD or Savior; and YOU will not give YOUR glory to another or YOUR praise to idols. Amen. THY throne O mighty GOD is in YOUR holy temple in the heaven of heavens where

The Disciples' Prayer

YOU wrap YOURSELF in an intensely bright and unapproachable light; YOU clothe YOURSELF with splendor (honor), power and majesty and YOU made the earth YOUR footstool. Amen. YOU O GOD, are the ultimate sovereign (supreme) ruler of the universe whose name is Yahweh (or Jehovah); YOU are *compassionate* (deep awareness of the suffering of others coupled with a strong desire and ability to relieve it) and *gracious* (characterized by undeserving kindness or benevolence and warm courtesy especially of a king to his subjects), *slow to anger*, abounding in *goodness* (excellent in preferring to choose right conduct or behavior over other competing alternatives) and *truth*, maintaining *love* (actively desiring all that is truly good for others) to thousands of generations that obey YOUR commandments and *forgiving* wickedness, rebellion and sin. Amen. Yet YOU do not leave the guilty unpunished; YOU punish the children to the third and fourth generations if they continue in the sins of their fathers. Amen. YOU do not permit the son to suffer for the iniquity of the father, nor the father to suffer for the sins of the son because YOU credit the righteousness of the righteous to the righteous and the wickedness of the wicked YOU charge against the wicked. Amen (Deu. 4:35; 33:39; Isa. 41:4; 42:8; 43:10-12; 44:6-8; 45:5-6, 21-23; 46:9-10; 48:12-13; Rom. 14:11; Rev. 1:8; Psa. 93:1; 104:1; 47:8; 103:19: Isa. 66:1; Dan. 7:9; Mat. 5:35; Acts 7:49; Exo. 34:5-7; Ezek. 18:20).

We confess that YOU are our heavenly Father because from one man (Adam) YOU made every nation of humans and YOU have actively been adopting us as sons and daughters through YOUR spirit (the spiritual or invisible gene or program) that indwells us and which continues to transform us into YOUR image and the exact likeness of Yehshua the Messiah (Jesus Christ), YOUR only begotten Son and our Redeemer. Amen. On the authority of Yehshua's (Jesus') acceptable sacrifice and our unshakeable trust in Him, we

The Disciples' Prayer

ask that our prayers may ascend before YOUR throne of grace like the distinctive, pleasant and sweet smell (aroma) of an acceptable offering and that YOU may grant all our requests for the sake of who YOU are and for the greater glory of YOUR name. Amen (Gen. 10:25; Joh. 3:8; Acts 17:28; Rom. 8:29; Gal. 3:26; Eph. 4:7-8, 11-12; 1 Joh. 3:9; Gen. 8:21; Rev. 5:8).

Hallowed be Thy Name

<u>Creative Power and Goodness</u>: We worship YOU O LORD our GOD (Yahweh-eloheenu or Jehovah-eloheenu), the GOD of all creation (Yahweh-elohim or Jehovah-elohim), because YOU command it and because YOU are the <u>only</u> One deserving of it. Amen. YOUR original creation was ruined (or marred) by the angelic rebellion in eternity past, and the earth became an empty wasteland without form, enveloped in deep darkness and the waters stood above the mountains. But because YOU originally created the earth to be inhabited, YOU decided to recreate it by the inimitable power of YOUR Word. Amen. YOU spoke, and immediately the deep darkness fled and a properly proportioned and perfectly blended mixture of gases (the atmosphere) enveloped the earth. Amen. YOU designed the properties and proportions of these gases in the atmosphere in such a way as to ensure and sustain the processes of life on earth. Amen. We highly exalt YOU on account of YOUR awesome power of creation, for YOU recreated the earth as a dazzling, azure (sky blue)-jewel, freely floating in space, and this event was so magnificent that all the Angels sang and shouted for joy. Amen. YOU placed the earth in the center of the galactic habitable zone, shielded from hostile regions within the galaxy, so that it will be perpetually habitable. Amen. The works of YOUR hands O GOD of all creation

The Disciples' Prayer

are awesome and in unsearchable wisdom YOU made the earth; continue to reveal to our minds the deep wonders of YOUR creation, so as to deepen and make perfect our fear of YOU. Amen (1 Chr. 16:29; Mat. 4:9-10; Gen. 1:1-2; Psa. 104:6; 111:10; Isa. 45:18; Heb. 11:3; Job 26:7; 28:28; 38:4-7; Pro. 1:7; 9:10; 15:33).

We greatly revere YOU because by the power of YOUR Word YOU also spoke into existence two universal (or global) floodlights; YOU made the universal furnace and daytime floodlight (the <u>sun</u>) to govern the day and to illuminate the face of the earth with its effulgent (radiant) glory so that nothing escapes its heat. Amen. YOU made the night-time floodlight (the <u>moon</u>) to govern the night by shedding its soft and subdued light when most of creation turn in for a night's repose. Amen. In obedience to YOUR everlasting command the heavenly bodies (the sun, moon and stars) continue to match with unequaled precision in their appointed paths; YOU set them in the sky as the earth's perfect timepieces that never need to be adjusted or repaired and to mark the length of the day, the month, the seasons and the year. Amen. We exceedingly adore YOU because by the power of YOUR Word, YOU rebuked the waters that covered the face of the earth and they fled; at the thunder of YOUR voice they took to flight and rushed off with a deafening roar to the place YOU assigned for them; YOU set a boundary they can never cross and never again will they cover the earth. Amen. YOU laid up the world's water supply in great reservoirs or storehouses (oceans, seas, lakes, etc.). Amen. We honor YOU exceedingly because YOU gave majestic form and graceful shape to the face of the earth by covering it with gorgeous mountains, hills, plateaus, valleys and ravines. Amen. In the magnificence of YOUR generosity, YOU buried beneath the earth treasures of all kinds of wealth for humanity; YOU filled the earth's bosom with deposits of minerals, metals, chemicals and other resources that would respond to the touch of humanity. Amen. O most wise GOD, how magnificent are the works of YOUR hands; with impeccable insight YOU created the earth; continue to reveal to our minds the deep secrets of YOUR creation, so as to deepen and make perfect our praise of YOU. Amen. (Gen. 1:9-10; 8:21-22; 1:14-18; Psa. 19:1-6; 33:7; 104:3-9).

We exceedingly adore and praise YOU because YOU spoke, and a beautiful, living, self-repairing, green carpet covered the face of the earth. Amen. With perfect artistic ingenuity, YOU chose to cover the earth with the color of green, a color that is soothing to the nerves and uplifting to the human spirit. Amen. YOU decorated this fascinating carpet with exquisitely colorful flowers for our appreciation and pleasure because they delight our senses. Amen. Though plants are sedentary and incapable of scouting for nourishment, YOU designed them with the ability not only to feed themselves, but to also feed other forms of life; YOU made them the primary producers of food for the whole of YOUR creation. Amen. We recognize YOUR loving care as our Provider because YOU prepared and packaged all the nutrients essential for the development and maintenance of strong, healthy bodies in the endless variety of fruits, nuts, tubers, grains and vegetables [we see growing in abundance around us]. Amen. YOU designed the outline of these plants so as to give the impression that they stand with outstretched arms of branches in continuous worship of their maker. Amen. We glorify YOUR magnificent name because YOUR creation of plants gives us a lucid illustration of how to be completely dependent on Yehshua (Jesus) for spiritual growth and fruitfulness even as branches are to the root; and the sowing, germination (or sprouting) and dispersal of seeds vividly remind us of the death and resurrection of Yehshua (Jesus) and of the life-transforming power of YOUR Word. Amen (Gen. 1:11-13; Joh. 15:1-7; Rom. 11:16-24).

The Disciples' Prayer

In a marvelous and ingenious manner, YOU contrived the creation of aerodynamic (or flying) animals (birds) and spoke them into existence. Amen. YOU designed their streamlined bodies and adorned them with lightness, smoothness and warmth; YOU adorned some with gorgeous and colorful plumage and to others YOU gave the ability to delight our ears with their singing. Amen. YOU gave the songbirds vocal ability to produce a variety of complex musical notes; YOU made them the world's master singers from whom we may learn the basic principles of good songs. Amen. With the help of their vigorous wings and rudder-like tails, YOU designed birds to overcome the force of gravity, to rise and poise themselves high amid the clouds, to glide motionless on a current of air or skim the surface of the deep, to sport with (or tease) the force and fury of the storm and move with ease and rapidity in whatever direction and at whatever speed they desire. Amen (Gen. 1:20-23).

YOU spoke, and many running waters became happy homes for diverse sea plants and fishes of every size, form and color. Amen. YOU designed the streamlined form of fishes and clothed them with scales (instead of feathers) and fins (in place of wings). Amen. With the aid of their fins and powerful tails, YOU designed them with the ability to swim swiftly and gracefully in water with their eyes wide open; YOU made them to be perfectly adapted to living in water. Amen. Beneath the surface of tropical waters, YOU designed the garden of delights (or submarine gardens) as a wonderland where we behold a spellbinding panoramic (constantly changing scene) view of beautiful forests of tree-like ocean plants, standing tall and erect, weaving to-and-fro in the ocean currents (much as pine trees bend and sway in the summer breezes) with myriads of beautifully colored, self-indulgent fishes that gambol (or frolic) in the shadows or bask (warm themselves) in the sun. Amen. With scientific ingenuity YOU reproduced YOUR creation on land in the

The Disciples' Prayer

seas. Amen. No wonder YOU inspired the Psalmist to write that those who go down to the seas, see YOUR great works and YOUR wonders in the deep. Amen. Our observation of the birds and fishes, make us feel envious because they make us yearn for the ecstatic freedom they display, their lack of lacking and the reckless abandonment with which they enjoy all that YOU have provided them. Amen. YOU O GOD are the Artist of Artists, the Scientist of Scientists, the Designer of Designers and Engineer of Engineers; help us to acquire much wisdom, understanding and insight from YOUR creation of the worlds of plants, birds and fishes, so as to deepen and make perfect our worship of YOU. Amen (Psa. 107:23-24; Job 12:7-9).

We give YOU glory and honor because YOU spoke and the earth was transformed into a global zoo comprising a plethora of diverse creeping and four-limbed animals. Amen. YOU designed each land animal with the abilities and physical attributes necessary to survive the challenges and demands of their everyday existence. Amen. YOUR creation of these animals is not indiscriminate (or haphazard) for each of them has a gospel for us. Amen. On account of YOUR infinite goodness, YOU crowned YOUR creation by creating the human race; YOU wonderfully and fearfully made us in YOUR image and likeness; YOU made us a little lower than the angels and crowned us with much glory and honor. Amen. YOU placed us on this exquisitely prepared earth and made us rulers over the works of YOUR hands; YOU put all things under our feet for our enjoyment (entertainment, nourishment and enlightenment) and unlike all other creatures, YOU gave us the ability to become like YOU by passionately seeking an intimate relationship with YOU. Amen. YOU created us and invited us to form with YOU a family of sinless, immortal humans for eternity. Amen. With majestic splendor, YOU spoke the whole of creation into existence by the inimitable power of YOUR Word and

The Disciples' Prayer

it was done; YOU commanded and it stood fast. Amen. The invisible power of YOUR Word became manifested as the visible creation that we are part of. Amen. We honor YOU because in spite of YOUR incomprehensible greatness, YOU still desire to have an experiential relationship with mere human mortals; what inexplicable humility, O great GOD. Let YOUR creation, most awesome GOD, continue to enlighten us in wisdom, understanding and insight so that we may continue to increasingly appreciate and comprehend YOUR creation; and continue to guide us into fulfilling the unique purpose of our creation. Amen (Gen. 1:24-26; Psa. 8:3-9; 33:9; 139:13-16; Jer. 10:12).

    The whole of creation (land, wind, water, sun, moon, stars, plants, birds, fishes and land animals) never cease to worship YOU O mighty GOD, because they never fail to do what YOU created them to do. Amen. YOU sustain the universe in perfect harmony through the power of YOUR Word, manifested (or revealed) as natural (physical, chemical and biological) or spiritual laws and principles. Amen. With perfect biologic, chemical and engineering ingenuity YOU made both plants and animals, and out of the abundance of YOUR loving-kindness, YOU satisfy the needs of each one of YOUR creation. Amen. By the inimitable power of YOUR Word, YOU made the flames of fire (the sun) YOUR faithful servants to purify and evaporate, through their heat, the earth's reservoir waters into vapor, which YOU designed to be stored in the clouds (water chariots). Amen. YOU command these water chariots to ride on the wings of YOUR messengers (the wind) over panting earth and as they lose heat, they unload their priceless cargoes of life-giving moisture over thirsty land. Amen. YOU cause this work to continue uninterrupted and so silently, so gently and so unobserved; and YOU inspired the Philosopher (or Preacher) to write that though the rains continue to pour, the seas are never full because the water returns to where it came from. Amen. YOU water the lands from YOUR upper chambers (the firmament or sky) and the earth is satisfied by the fruit of YOUR work; YOU quench the thirst of all animals, the birds nest by the waters and sing among the branches; YOU make the grass to grow for the cattle and YOU cause humans to cultivate the land to bring forth wine that gladdens our hearts, oil to make our skin glow and food that nourishes our bodies. Amen. When we ponder YOUR creation of sleep and wakefulness, we are reminded that at the end of our earthly sojourn, physical death awaits us, after which comes the resurrection. Amen. All of YOUR animate creation look up to YOU for their needs and in YOUR infinite wisdom, YOU already set in motion self-sustaining processes that will always have their needs met and YOU equipped them with the innate ability to obtain nourishment from their immediate environment, providentially stocked with foods in abundance. Amen (Psa. 104:3-4; Eccl. 1:7; 1 Cor. 15:20-22; 42-43; 51-53; Psa. 104:10-17; 27-29).

When we consider the harmony and diversity within YOUR creation, the uniqueness and design of each organism, the interdependence between organisms and the problem-solving design that runs through the whole of YOUR creation, we feel inconsequential, infinitesimal and overwhelmed with wonderment. Amen. Whether we view the world beneath us or scan the starry heavens above us, we constantly behold YOUR eternal power and irrefutable deity being made visible in creation, so that we cannot claim to be ignorant of YOU. Amen. Continue to reveal to us the true knowledge of YOUR creation and grant us an ever-increasing appreciation of it so as to fill us with a worshipful spirit and a grateful heart. Amen (Rom. 1:20).

<u>Holiness</u>: We revere YOU O LORD, the GOD who sanctifies us (Yahweh-Mekaddishkem or Jehovah-Mekaddishkem) because of YOUR awesome holiness. Amen. YOU O GOD,

are majestic and perfect in holiness; none is holy like YOU; YOUR name is holy, YOUR words are holy and YOU are so holy that YOU can neither behold evil nor look upon iniquity. Amen. YOU gave the Israelites ritualistic (or ceremonial) cleansing (or washing) rites to impress upon their hearts that YOU are a holy (spiritually clean) GOD who demands holiness from YOUR true worshippers. Amen. Because of YOUR holiness, YOU hate sin with perfect hatred, YOUR whole being reacts against it and YOU can neither dwell with nor have fellowship with sinners; in fact YOUR undiluted wrath is upon all unrepentant sinners. Amen. YOU are infinitely holy because each of YOUR attributes excels in excellence and cannot be improved upon; and before sinners can come into YOUR presence and have fellowship with YOU, we must be acquitted of our condemnation by being clothed with the perfect righteousness that comes through faith in Yehshua (Jesus) and with a wholehearted yieldedness to the leading of the holy spirit. Amen. Continue to teach us to joyfully and proudly praise and adore YOU on account of YOUR holiness as is being done by the angelic hosts in heaven and continue to sanctify us until we become as perfect as YOU and Yehshua (Jesus). Amen (Ex. 15:11; 1 Sam. 2:2; Isa. 57:15; Jer. 23:9; Luke 1:49; Lev. 11:44-45; 19:2; 20:7, 26; 1 Pet. 1:15-16; Psa. 5:4-6; Isa. 59:2; Nah. 1:2; Hab. 1:13; Rom. 1:18; Psa. 30:4; Isa. 6:3; Mat. 5:48; Rom. 12:1; 1 Thes. 4:7; Heb. 12:14; Rev. 4:8).

Righteousness and Justice: We worship YOU most just Judge and the GOD of our righteousness (Yahweh-Tsidkeenu or Jehovah-Tsidkeenu) because of YOUR impeccable uprightness and justice, and because in YOU there is no favoritism or partiality. Amen. Since YOU are infinitely holy, YOU cannot be indifferent to sin and refuse to manifest YOUR severity toward it; if YOU fail to give sin (the rejection of YOUR revealed way of life) its full measure of punish-

The Disciples' Prayer

ment, then YOU would be acting contrary to YOUR revealed nature and cannot claim to be perfectly just and holy. Amen. We adore YOU because YOUR perfect justice demands that the just penalty for sin is death and in YOUR excellence YOU swore by YOUR eternal self to punish YOUR enemies who hate YOU because they neither give heed to YOUR Word nor walk according to YOUR commandments. Amen. We eulogize YOUR righteousness and justice because YOU have not kept them a secret from us but have continued to manifest them in YOUR dealings with YOUR arch-enemy Satan, and with sinful and obedient humans. Amen (Deu. 32:40-42; Rom. 12:19).

As the ultimate Judge of the whole earth, YOUR impartiality and incorruptibility is immeasurable, YOUR legal honesty to all of YOUR creation cannot be improved upon and YOUR actions conform to the strictest legal requirements of justice ever known since the beginning of the world. Amen. Since true justice is impossible without just judgment, YOU established YOUR Word as the standard against which all of mankind will be judged. We exceedingly revere YOU because YOU have continued to reveal a flawless consistency in YOUR judgments against sin throughout the course of man's history, as revealed by YOUR pronouncements of the death sentence, the curse on the earth, the worldwide deluge, the localized and utter destruction of the cities of Sodom and Gomorrah, YOUR severe judgment against the gods of Egypt and the Egyptians; YOUR numerous judgments against YOUR chosen nation Israel, including their banishment from the Promised Land into exile; and even the forsaking and death of Yehshua (Jesus) while He bore our sins on the cross. Amen. YOUR wrath against sin is not the impulsive outburst of YOUR holy anger aimed capriciously (whimsically) at people whom YOU do not like; it is YOUR eternal detestation of all unrighteousness; it is YOUR righteous displeasure and the indignation of YOUR justice against evil; it is YOUR holiness stirred into activity against sin and the just sentence which YOU decreed upon evil doers. Amen. We pray that YOU may continue to impress upon our minds the extreme horror of YOUR wrath against sin, so as not to be prone to regard it lightly, or to gloss over its hideousness or make excuses for it; and to fervently praise YOU because YOU have delivered us from YOUR awful wrath to come. Amen (Gen. 18:25; Psa. 36:6; 89:14; 103:6; Isa. 5:16; Jer. 9:24; Gen. 2:16-17; 3:17-18, 23; 6:5-8; 7:11-12; 19:23-25; Exo. 7:8-14:31; Psa. 78:8-68; 105-106; Neh. 9:6-36; Heb. 3:8-11; Mat. 27:46; 1 Thes. 1:10).

In the same manner and with irreproachable constancy YOU have shown mercy and favor to many Ancestors of our Faith as revealed by YOUR deliverance of Noah (a preacher of righteousness) and his family from the world-wide deluge; the enormous material blessing of Abraham; the banishment of the shame of barrenness from Sarah, Rebecca, Rachel, Hannah and Elizabeth; YOUR merciful deliverance of righteous Lot from the destruction of Sodom and Gomorrah because of his continuous torment by the immoral and outrageous behavior of his neighbors; the supernatural deliverance of Israel from their enslavement in Egypt; the gift of the Promised Land (Canaan) to the nation of Israel; the exaltation (or elevation) of the Patriarch Joseph from enslavement and imprisonment to royalty; the generous restoration of the Patriarch Job who suffered terribly though he was righteous; the revelation of deep secrets (or mysteries) to Joseph and Daniel; the incredible deliverance of the three Jews (Shadrach, Meshach and Abednego) from the fiery furnace; the miraculous deliverance of Daniel from the den of lions; the healing of diverse sicknesses and illnesses and the casting out of demons by Yehshua (Jesus) and our Apostolic Fathers and the glorious exaltation of Yehshua (Jesus) our Lord and Savior. Amen. We pray that these benevolent acts of YOURS would be indelibly etched in our hearts so that they may be

The Disciples' Prayer

our sources of encouragement and comfort and of our absolute conviction that YOU are a GOD whose eyes are continuously upon those who sincerely seek YOU and YOUR ears always attentive to those who truly depend on YOU. Amen (Gen. 6:9, 17-19; 8:18-19; 13:2; 25:1-4; 21:1-3; 25:21-23; 30:1-2, 22-24; 1 Sam. 1:5-8, 19-20; Lk. 1:5-7, 11-17, 24-25; Gen. 18: 20-21; 19:12-29; 2 Pet. 2:7-8; Exo. 3:1-14:31; Jos. 21:43-45; Gen. 37:28; 39:19-20; 41:39-44; Job 1:13-22; 2:7; 42:10-17; Gen. 37:5-10; 40:8-23; 41:15-32; Dan. 2:17-45; 4:18-28; 5:13-17, 24-31; 3:13-27; 6:16-30; Mat. 4:24; Luke. 9:1-2; Acts 19:11-12; Mk. 16:19; Phil. 2:9-11).

Most righteous GOD, among all of YOUR creation, Lucifer was most capable of perceiving YOUR nature and goodness, having been created as the epitome (or model) of perfection; he was close enough to being like YOU that he thought equality with YOU was something he could grab. Amen. When he eventually sinned by desiring to usurp YOUR authority, YOU restrained YOURSELF by postponing the implementation of the ultimate penalty for his sin to the distant future but banished (or exiled) him from YOUR presence to await the execution of YOUR judgment. Amen. If YOU had immediately annihilated him from existence, the angelic hosts (or inhabitants of heaven) lacking in the experiential knowledge of the consequences of sin could not have seen YOUR justice and righteousness in his destruction and they would have served YOU from fear. Amen. Since YOUR desire is for all intelligences (beings) to worship YOU out of genuine love instead of fear, their loyalty (or allegiance) must rest upon an immovable assuredness (or certitude) in YOUR justice and benevolence. Amen. In YOUR infinite wisdom therefore, YOU decided that for the ultimate good of the universe, Satan must not be restrained from expounding his evil principles so that all beings would bear witness to the ugly consequences of rejecting YOUR divine authority, thereby forever placing YOUR justice, righteousness and the immutability (unchangeableness) of YOUR law beyond all question. Amen. We are full of admiration for YOUR enormous restraint even when dealing with YOUR arch-enemy and for YOUR unfathomable wisdom and incalculable insight in putting the overall good of the universe above all other considerations, and pray that YOU may abundantly endow us with these attributes. Amen (Isa. 14:12-14; Ezek. 28:11-17; Phil. 2:6-11; Rev. 12:7-12; 20:1-3, 10).

Most awesome GOD, at creation, YOU gave our first parents unlimited dominion (or authority) over all the earth as long as they remained obedient to YOUR instructions. Amen. Even Satan and his demons were subject to the authority of the first humans; but out of spite for YOU and envy for the honored position YOU showered upon our first parents, Satan deceived them into disobeying the commandment that YOU gave them for our eternal good, thereby derailing YOUR purpose for the creation of humanity. Amen. YOU gave us the freedom of choice to choose between a GOD-dependent (theocentricism; i.e. depending on YOU to regulate our way of life) or self (or human)-centered (anthropocentrism; i.e. depending on our limited abilities to determine our way of life) rulership, but our first parents chose to reject YOUR truth that was essential for our eternal life and accepted Satan's lies. Amen. Unfortunately, each of us that has ever lived has been presented with the same option as our first parents, and we followed in their footstep; each one of us by our personal choices indicated our preference to be Satan's slaves so that we have always lived according to his standard. Amen. By virtue of our voluntary act of disobedience to YOUR revealed way of life, the entire human race became destined to learn by personal experience the consequences of self-rulership, instead of GOD-rulership which only requires us to completely put our trust in YOUR instruction, guidance and help. Amen. As the immediate consequence of this fall, the whole of humanity lost the blissful fellowship we were created to enjoy with YOU, our original authority over the earth was transferred to Satan, and we became subjected to his authority and to death. Amen (Gen. 1:28-30; 2:15-17; 3:1-6; Rom. 5:12; 1 Cor. 15:21-22; Gen. 3:22-24; Rom. 6:16; 8:5-7).

YOU mercifully drove them (i.e. the first humans) out of the Garden of Eden because if they had eaten of the fruit of life, they would have become immortal without the opportunity for repentance and salvation. Amen. The outcome of these events was not in the best interest of YOUR creation because as long as the authority (legal right to administer the earth) was in the hands of condemned sinners (fallen angels), YOUR creation was in danger of annihilation. Amen. Just as YOU decided to recreate the earth after its ruination by Lucifer's sin, in the same manner, YOU decided to reverse this status quo, and the only viable solution out of this predicament was the righteous and just retrieval of the authority by an upright sinless human, but there was none in all the earth. Amen. If YOU had destroyed our first parents, it would not have changed the state of affairs since the authority was no longer in their hands. Amen. We glorify and honor YOU for being so self-controlled in the face of such a colossal betrayal and for focusing on a remedy instead of the offense; and pray that YOU input in us these admirable attributes. Amen (Gen. 3:22-24).

To bring about the dethronement of Satan without offending YOUR perfect righteousness and justice, YOU created a second Adam that was as perfect as the first Adam (before his fall) and YOU named him Yehshua (Jesus). Amen. Because of his sinlessness and a lifetime of overcoming temptations by his complete submission to YOUR authority, Yehshua (Jesus) legally satisfied all YOUR righteous and just requirements for the transfer of authority and actually earned the righteousness that the first Adam was conferred with but squandered, thereby making possible the legal transfer of authority from Satan to Him and the re-establishment of the blissful fellowship we were created to enjoy with YOU. Amen. We adore and glorify YOU for not contradicting YOUR moral standards as YOU sought to bring forth an eternal and enduring solution to humanity's betrayal; and pray YOU to endow us with such unwavering constancy in our character. Amen (Gen. 3:15; Rom. 5:15-17; 1 Cor. 15:45; Heb. 2:18; 4:15; Phil. 2:8).

GOD of justice and righteousness, even with the transfer of authority from Satan to Yehshua (Jesus), we sometimes feel depressed and discouraged because of the prevalence and profundity of inequity and injustice that continues to flourish on earth as it has always been and this makes it very challenging for us to continue to be submissive to YOU when those who do otherwise appear to live a better life. Amen. Good LORD, how do we rationalize the fact that the wicked sometimes have a disproportionately greater share of outward prosperity; they seem to have the least share of troubles in this life and seem to have the greatest share of its comforts; they live without due regard for YOU, yet they prosper. Most merciful GOD, such musings (meditations) sorely stretch our faith to breaking point; they are fierce storms that strain the firmest anchors of our faith, but we trust that Yehshua (Jesus) will continue to quell the storms in our lives. Amen. YOU are definitely not indifferent to our miseries, for in actuality it breaks YOUR heart to see us in the spiritual squalor in which we live, hence YOU gave YOUR only begotten Son as an assurance that YOU are in the trenches with us. Amen (Psa. 37:1-6; 73; Jer. 12:1; Hab. 1:2-4; Mk. 4:37-41; Lk. 8:23-25).

O GOD our righteousness, we glorify YOUR wonderful name because Yehshua's (Jesus') kingdom is not of the present world system but will be established at His second coming during which time His authority will be in full effect and the fruits of His righteous government will be mani-

The Disciples' Prayer

fested. Amen. Most awesome GOD of our righteousness, we praise YOUR mighty name because during this waiting (or transitory) period, YOU are actively calling out faithful and loyal co-rulers and co-heirs from the kingdom of darkness to the kingdom of YOUR Son. Amen. Because YOU are a GOD that is transparently honest, YOU warned us that the life path that will be trodden by these called-out ones will be unpopular and arduous. Amen. We glorify YOUR most righteous name because the sufferings and adversities we go through do not come from YOU, but are the fruits of the reign of sin in a fallen world and the direct results of the wrath of Satan against all Believers. Amen. Even the whole of creation groans with us as a woman in labor (with birth pangs), in eager expectation of the appearance of the kingdom of light. Amen (Dan. 7:13-14; Joh. 18:36; Rev. 11:15; 19:11-16, 19-20:4; Acts 26:18: 1 Col. 1:13; 1 Pet. 2:9; Mat. 7:13-14; Joh. 14:1, 27; 15:18-21; 16:33; 17:14-16; Acts 14:22; Joh. 15:18-21; Rev. 12:17; Rom. 8:19-23).

We exalt and praise YOUR holy name because no matter our circumstances, YOU have given us everything we need for life and godliness, and because YOUR eyes are constantly upon us and YOUR ears always attentive to our prayers. Amen. We thank YOU for YOUR fatherly discipline because YOU use our peculiar situations to build spiritual character in us suitable for kingdom living, thereby demonstrating to us that we are not YOUR illegitimate children (or bastards). Amen. We thank YOU because we are comforted by the persuasion that in enduring these hardships we follow in the footsteps of Yehshua (Jesus) and the Saints and that these sufferings are an assurance that we would share in the glorification of Yehshua (Jesus). Amen. We praise and honor YOU because these hardships and sufferings will motivate us to pray more fervently for the establishment of the fullness of YOUR kingdom. Amen. Since no eye has seen, nor ear heard, nor mind conceived what YOU are preparing for us, we are more determined to endure the sufferings of the present time since they would be nothing compared to the glory that awaits us. Amen. We glorify YOU because we are convinced beyond any reasonable doubts that our genuine desire for egalitarianism and bliss cannot be actualized apart from YOU, and this vindicates YOU because YOU knew all along that the consequences of our anthropocentric (or self-directed) choice will be too traumatic for us. Amen. Let us be firmly rooted in the conviction that YOU are unequalled in the deliverance of the righteous from adversities and the preservation of the ungodly for the ultimate punishment when the full fury of YOUR wrath will be unleashed upon them; and empower us with all that is necessary to continue to defend YOUR perfect righteousness and justice in the knowledge of the truth and with boldness. Amen (2 Pet. 1:3-4; 1 Pet. 3:12; Pro. 3:11-12; 2 Cor. 12:7-10; Heb. 12:5-11; 2 Pet. 1:3-4; Rom. 8:17; Isa. 64:4; 1 Cor. 2:9; Joh. 15:18-21; Dan. 2:44; Rev. 12:12).

Love and Compassion: We adore YOU O GOD because of YOUR unfathomable love, compassion and mercy for the human race. Amen.

After the fall of humanity, the inherent nature of all things became corrupted so that we became carnally minded, incapable of submitting to YOUR commandments and consequently became YOUR fierce enemies. Amen. But because of YOUR solicitude, indescribable love and incomprehensible mercy for the human race and in spite of our animosity toward YOU, YOU decided to redeem us so that we may be able to fulfill the original purpose for which we were created. Amen. Even while we were YOUR acrimonious enemies, YOU devised an eternal plan that will reconcile us to YOU through YOUR only begotten Son, Yehshua (Jesus). Amen. YOU sent Him to the earth to reveal YOUR plan to acquit us

The Disciples' Prayer

of the rightly deserved death sentence that was hanging over our heads. Amen.

We were like condemned, unremorseful (or unrepentant) spiritual criminals awaiting the implementation of the death sentence against us when YOU, the ultimate Judge of the universe, decided to grant us a conditional pardon (or acquittal) without our appealing against YOUR just judgment. Amen. The only condition was that a sinless substitute had to die in our place before our acquittal could be effected, and since YOUR only begotten Son was the only sinless substitute in all of creation, YOU willingly gave Him up to die in our place that we may live. Amen. Broken-heartedly, YOU gave up the only being that had the most intimate relationship with YOU to save YOUR enemies. Amen. As if these were not enough, as the GOD with unlimited power, YOU promised us that at our acquittal, YOU will do everything within YOUR power to ensure that our new life will be like that of YOUR only begotten Son. Amen. O most loving and compassionate GOD, this kind of love is too profound for our comprehension because though it is conceivable to die for a friend, it is absolutely unthinkable to die for an enemy. Amen (Joh. 3:16; Rom. 5:8; 8:7).

We hail and honor Yehshua (Jesus), our Lord and Savior, for this expression of unfathomable love for us and we venerate Him for being obedient to YOU in all things to ensure the unveiling of this salvation plan. Amen. We cannot thank YOU sufficiently for not sparing YOUR only Son from death for our sake and for giving us this second chance to fulfill the eternal purpose of our creation. Amen. Since both of YOU first demonstrated YOUR profound love for us when we were so undeserving, only both of YOU are worthy of our genuine love because no one living or dead can ever come close to loving us as YOU have loved us. Amen. We beseech YOU to establish with us the most loving, permanent and experiential relationship of foremost and absolute intimacy with YOU and with Yehshua the Messiah (Jesus Christ) that will be incomparably superior to any other relationship ever formed in our present lifetime. Amen. Let nothing separate us from the love of the Messiah (Christ); let neither suffering, nor afflictions, nor tribulations, nor calamities, nor distress, nor persecution, nor hunger, nor destitution, nor peril, nor the sword separate us from the love of Him who gave His life for us. Amen. Let neither death nor life, nor angels, nor principalities, nor powers, nor things impending and threatening, nor things to come, nor height, nor depth, nor anything else in all creation separate us from YOUR love for us. Amen. We pray that YOU abundantly endow us with YOUR attributes of altruistic love, mercy and benevolence and empower us to bestow these on those who are undeserving so that we may love as YOU have loved us. Amen (Isa. 53:3; Joh. 5:23; Phil. 2:8-9; 1 Joh. 4:19; 5:13; Rom. 8:38, 38-39).

Faithfulness and Mercy: We wholeheartedly adore YOU because YOU are faithful to all YOUR promises and YOU are the only dependable being worthy of our trust; blessed be YOUR glorious name, and may it be exalted above all blessing and praise. Amen. YOU called out the father of our faith (Patriarch Abram) from his father's household, made a covenant with him and his descendants and prospered him exceedingly according to YOUR promises. Amen. True to YOUR promises, YOU heard the cry of his descendants in Egyptian bondage and through Moses, YOU pronounced severe judgments against the Egyptians and their gods. Amen. YOU demonstrated that no god, king or nation could withstand YOUR awesome power; YOU destroyed the land of Egypt and the military might of the greatest kingdom on earth (superpower) at that time; palpable fear and terror gripped the hearts of all their neighbors who had seen and heard of YOUR mighty deeds; and with great power YOU

The Disciples' Prayer

brought Israel out of Egypt as a wealthy nation. Amen. YOU intended that this new nation was to be YOUR earthly kingdom and a theocratic state with YOU as their King, and through them, YOU purposed to reveal YOURSELF to the whole world. Amen. We praise and glorify YOUR most blessed name because there is no god like YOU; YOU are awesome in power, majestic in glory and faithful to YOUR promises. Amen (Psa. 33:4; 145:13; 1 Thes. 5:24; Heb. 10:23; Gen. 12:1-3, 7; 13:2; 15:2-21; 16:16; 17:1-22; 25:1-2, 5-6; Exo. 7:8-12:30; 13:17-14:31; 15:11-16; Psa. 78:1-13; 42-53; 105:1-38; 106:6-12; Neh. 9:8-12; Ezek. 20:2-10).

In their journey to the Promised Land (Canaan), YOU protected Israel, YOU fed her with the food of angels and quenched her thirst by causing water to gush out from the rock; YOU established a covenant with her and appealed to her to keep YOUR regulations and commandments; YOU set before Israel the choice of either life and prosperity or death and destruction; and entreated her to choose life. Amen. Most loving GOD, in YOUR dealings with Israel YOU came across as a newly wed that appeared intoxicated with spousal love. Amen. But in spite of all these, Israel consistently flaunted her distrust in YOU; she attributed her deliverance from slavery to a lifeless idol; she constantly whined and repeatedly expressed her preference to go back into slavery in Egypt. Amen. For forty years YOU sustained the Israelites in the desert and put up with their rebellion; they lacked nothing, their clothes did not wear out, nor did their feet become swollen; and because of the promises YOU made to Abraham, YOU did not utterly destroy rebellious Israel in the desert. Amen. We praise and glorify YOUR most blessed name because YOU are most merciful, most gracious and full of compassion; YOU are a forgiving GOD, slow to anger and abounding in love. Amen (Exo. 9:1-29; 32:7-14; Deu. 30:15-20; Neh. 9:13-21; Psa. 78:17-41; 105:13-33; Ezek. 20:11-26).

YOU struck down the unbelieving elders of Israel so that they did not enter the Promised Land, but YOU made their sons as numerous as the stars in the sky, and YOU brought them into the land that YOU commanded their fathers to enter and possess. Amen. YOU subdued the physically-intimidating Canaanites before them; they captured large fortified cities they did not build; they took possession of houses filled with all kinds of good things they did not labor for; they inherited wells they did not dig and vineyards, olive groves and fruit trees they did not plant; they ate to their fill and were well nourished and reveled in YOUR great goodness. Amen. YOU were so anxious for Israel to walk according to YOUR laws so that YOU would manifest the depths of YOUR generosity to them, but they would not; YOU appealed to the young of Israel to keep YOUR commandments and to walk in YOUR ordinances, but they were as disobedient and rebellious as their fathers; so YOU handed them over to their enemies, who oppressed them. Amen. When they were chastised in this manner, they cried to YOU for deliverance, and in YOUR great compassion and because of the covenant YOU made with them, YOU rescued them from the hands of their enemies. Amen. But as soon as they were at rest, they would turn their backs to YOU; then YOU would abandon them to the hands of their enemies so that they ruled over them. Amen. For over three centuries (300 years), YOU continued to exercise enormous restraint during this cycle of willful rebellion, false repentance and forgiveness. Amen. We praise and glorify YOUR most blessed name because YOU are most merciful, most gracious and full of compassion; YOU are a forgiving GOD, slow to anger and abounding in loving kindness; YOU are a GOD who jealously protects HIS integrity and who cannot renege on HIS promises. Amen (Deu. 5:29; 6:10-12; Jos. 21:43-45; 23:14; Psa. 78:54-59; 81:13; 106:34-46; Isa. 48:18-19; Neh. 9:22-31).

The Disciples' Prayer

When they rejected YOUR (heavenly) sovereignty mediated through YOUR prophets and demanded earthly kings like the surrounding nations, YOU mercifully granted them their hearts' desires. Amen. Because King David was very zealous in YOUR service YOU established a covenant with him, but Israel later became idolatrous and was led astray. Amen. On account of their spiritual promiscuity, YOU tore Israel (Samaria) away from the House of David (Judah), but Samaria (ten tribes of Israel) persisted in doing great evil in YOUR sight and provoked YOU to anger; she indulged in every evil thing YOU had warned against and did not heed YOUR warnings through YOUR prophets. Amen. YOU even thought that after she was spent in her spiritual whoredom (idolatry), she would return to YOU, but she did not; so YOU removed her from YOUR presence by giving her a Certificate of Divorce and allowed her to be taken into captivity at the hands of her adulterous companion (the Assyrians). Amen. YOU had hoped that Judah (Southern Israel) would learn from her sister's fate, but surprisingly even she did not keep YOUR commands; and in spite of YOUR warnings through YOUR prophets, Judah did not return to YOU with all her heart, but only in pretence. Amen. Consequently, YOU also rejected Judah by giving her a Certificate of Separation and by permitting the destruction of YOUR beloved city (Jerusalem) and the leading of her remnant into Babylonian exile. Amen. We eulogize YOUR most loving nature because for approximately 3-4 centuries (300-400 years) YOU endured the repulsive behavior of the descendants of Abraham and the promiscuity of a people YOU loved like a spouse. Amen. We praise and glorify YOUR most blessed name because though YOU are most merciful, most gracious and full of compassion; and though YOU do not permit iniquity to go unpunished; YOUR judgments are perfectly just because YOU temper (or mitigate) justice with mercy. Amen (1 Sam. 8:4-9, 19-20; 2 Kgs. 17:6-

23; 2 Chr. 36:15-20; Ezra 9:6-15; Neh. 9:32-37; Jer. 3:7-10; 2:1-4:4; Ezek. 23:3-33).

In Babylonian exile, the House of David cried out to YOU for deliverance and because YOU are a covenant-keeping GOD, YOU remembered YOUR promises to Patriarchs Abraham and King David, and YOU made provisions for Judah's gradual return to Jerusalem and the neighboring towns. Amen. Over time, the Religious Leaders of this new Jewish nation became very corrupt and substituted the true requirements of YOUR Law with their man-made traditions. Amen. Therefore, at the fullness of time, YOU sent the expected Messiah (Christ) and YOUR only begotten Son to the Jews; and by the miracles, wonders and signs that YOU performed through Him, YOU were signaling to the Jewish leaders that Yehshua (Jesus) was the promised Messiah (Christ) sent by YOU. Amen. YOU had hoped that they would listen to Him, but like YOU predicted, they rejected Him; He was maltreated, abused and murdered; but YOU raised Him from the dead. Amen. In dying however, He inaugurated and ratified the New Covenant of Grace with the whole world and YOU bestowed upon Him all authority and power in heaven and on earth. Amen (Mat. 21:33-44; Joh. 5:36-38; 6:29; 10:27-29; Acts 2:22-24, 38; Heb. 7:18-22; 8:6-12; 10:16)

We bless and glorify YOUR awesome name because YOU had revealed that just as the nation of Israel provoked YOU to jealousy with her idolatry (spiritual adultery), so also will YOU provoke her to jealousy and to anger through the Gentiles. Amen. Because YOU held out YOUR outstretched hands unto a disobedient and obstinate people for centuries, YOU solemnly pledged that YOU will be found by those who did not seek YOU and that YOU will reveal YOURSELF to those who are undeserving of it. Amen. The indomitability of YOUR sovereignty is revealed by the fact that while humanity's Archenemy (Satan) was preoccupied with enticing Israel to rebel against YOU continually, little did he know that Israel's rebellion will lead to the ultimate redemption of the whole world (both Jews and Gentiles). Amen. Though YOU scattered the Jews throughout the world for killing YOUR only begotten Son, YOU also promised to restore them by granting them faith in the Messiah (Christ) and bringing them back to their land. Amen (Deu. 32:21; Isa. 65:1-2; Ezek. 36:16-38; Rom. 10:19-21).

We praise and adore YOU because YOUR Word reveals that the promises of this New Covenant are far superior to that made in the former, and that through this covenant, YOU will bring complete fulfillment to the promises of the Abrahamic and Davidic Covenants. Amen. We trust that YOU will fulfill YOUR promises because the whole of Scripture testifies to this immutability in YOUR nature; YOU remain faithful even when we are unfaithful because YOU cannot deny YOURSELF, but our earnest petition is that YOU empower us to keep our own end of this spiritual contract so that we will be grandiose beneficiaries of these magnificent promises. Amen (Job 42:2; Jer. 24:7; 32:40; Ezek. 11:19; 36:26; Mk. 16:16; Joh. 6:35, 40, 51, 53-58; 10:10; Rom. 8:28; 1 Cor. 10:13; 2 Cor. 1:20; Gal. 3:16; Phil. 4:19; 2 Tim. 2:13; 1 Thes. 5:24; Heb. 7:18-22; 13:5-6; 2 Pet. 1:4).

Omniscience: We greatly adore YOU because since YOU created all things YOUR knowledge of the universe is complete and cannot be improved upon. Amen. Apart from revealing YOURSELF in creation, YOU have always revealed YOURSELF personally to those who truly revere YOU. Amen. Because of the enormous fear associated with YOUR self-revelation, YOU have continued to reveal YOURSELF through YOUR chosen prophets, and through them, YOU have given absolute and irrefutable proof of YOUR existence through accurately fulfilled prophecies. Amen. Only the true GOD can accurately foretell scientific truths unknown at the time of revelation; perfectly foreknow the rise and fall of the empires of Babylon, Medo-Persia, Greece and Rome; accurately foretell the struggles between the Seleucid and Ptolemic dynasties; and also unmistakably prophesy specific and verifiable details concerning the birth, intense suffering and death of Yehshua the Messiah (Jesus Christ). Amen (Gen. 2:15-17; 3:2-3, 10; 4:5-7; 6:13; 7:5; 12:1, 7; 13:14; 17:1-3; Exo. 33:11; Deu. 5:4-5; Exo. 20:18-19; Isa. 46:9-10).

Most importantly however, because YOU are not a GOD who is shrouded in secrecy, YOU revealed YOUR redemptive plan for humanity in YOUR holy feasts. Amen. We exalt YOUR most awesome name for blessing us with the <u>weekly sabbath</u> as a symbol of the millennial reign of Yehshua (Jesus) over the earth; for giving us the <u>Passover</u> as a symbol of our deliverance from eternal death through the sacrificial death of Yehshua (Jesus) who is our Passover Lamb; and for furnishing us with the <u>feast of unleavened bread</u> as a symbol for the removal of the leaven of sin from our lives through Yehshua's (Jesus') sacrifice so that we may walk in His holiness. Amen. We shamelessly applaud YOU for giving us the <u>feast of Pentecost</u> as a symbol for the first fruits (or the little flock) of YOUR harvest as manifested in Yehshua's (Jesus') resurrection from the dead, His ascension into heaven and in the outpouring of the holy spirit on His Apostles and Disciples; for blessing us with the <u>feast of trumpets</u> which points to the second coming of Yehshua (Jesus) and the resurrection of the Saints; and for transmitting to us the <u>Day of Atonement</u> as a symbol of our eternal forgiveness (or cleansing from sin) and the removal of the influence of Satan (the author of sin) over the whole earth. Amen. We idolize YOU for giving us the <u>feast of the tabernacles</u> as a symbol of YOUR everlasting kingdom during which YOU will reign as King over us on earth and for furnishing us with the <u>last great day feast</u> as a symbol of

The Disciples' Prayer

the second resurrection and the final judgment (Great White Throne Judgment). Amen (Lev. 15:13; 17:11; 23:1-44; Job 26:7; Psa. 8:8; 34:20; Eccl. 1:6-7; Isa. 7:14; 40:22; 53; Ezek. 26:1-6; Dan. 7:1-8:26; 9:21-27; 11:2-12:4; Mic. 5:2; 1 Cor. 15:20; Heb. 4:4-11; Rev. 20-21).

We adore YOU because in all matters concerning YOUR redemptive plan or certain events that YOU have foreordained to occur, all YOUR prophetic revelations come true since they are based on YOUR absolute foreknowledge. Amen. We exalt YOUR wondrous name because in our personal lives, YOU choose not to exercise YOUR absolute foreknowledge; YOU choose to have an open-ended foreknowledge so as not to invalidate our freedom of choice. Amen. In such cases, YOU meekly hope that intelligent beings will respond in a manner that will glorify YOUR name. Amen. Continue to reveal YOURSELF to us until YOU bring us to the point of truly recognizing YOU for who YOU are and accept YOUR revealed knowledge and YOUR purpose for us. Amen. Help us to be passionate about not profaning (or tarnishing) YOUR awesome reputation and continue to glorify YOUR name by doing wondrous things in our lives that will far outstrip our wildest imaginations or dreams. Amen. Continue to make perfect in us a genuine spirit of praise and gratitude for who YOU truly are and continue to perfect us in our worship of YOU in truth and in spirit. Amen (Isa. 46:10-11; 48:3-5; Jer. 1:5; Rom. 8:29; Gal. 1:15-16; Gen. 22:10-12; Exo. 32:14; Deu. 8:2; Num. 14:11; 1 Sam. 13:13; 1 Kgs. 21:29; 2 Kgs. 20:5-6; Joh. 3:10).

(<u>Personal Praise and Thanksgiving:</u> Praise and thank GOD for specific things HE has done in YOUR life, the lives of family members, friends, etc).

Thy Kingdom come, Thy will be done on earth as is done in Heaven.

Kingdom Petition: We acknowledge YOU as our Sovereign GOD (Adonai-Yahweh or Adonai-Jehovah) and exceedingly eulogize YOUR most holy name for revealing to us that YOUR kingdom refers to the final vindication (or blamelessness) of YOUR purpose for creation, manifested in the outpouring of YOUR redemptive sovereignty for the destruction of Satan and all his works. Amen. We exalt YOUR awesome name for making us come to the knowledge that like any other kingdom, YOUR glorious kingdom will have a literal territory, a ruling king, inhabitants (or subjects) and laws that regulate the conduct of all that dwell within it. Amen. We adore YOU for making known to us that this kingdom will begin as the one thousand (1000) year Messianic reign of Yehshua (Jesus) and will culminate in YOUR golden and everlasting kingdom. Amen. We therefore pray that YOU hasten the establishment of this utopian kingdom that will destroy all pre-existing kingdoms of humanity with all their failed governmental structures (including education, health, economy, the judiciary, etc.). Amen. We strongly desire the establishment of this theocratic government that will be headquartered in

Jerusalem (YOUR beloved city) and in which Yehshua the Messiah (Jesus Christ) will be our King, Judge and High Priest; we pray for the inauguration of this government in which impartiality, fairness and true justice will reign because Yehshua (Jesus) and His Cabinet of victorious Saints will judge the nations with righteousness and equity; they will gently correct the meek, rebuke the oppressors of the earth and destroy the wicked. Amen. We yearn for the enthronement of this government wherein Yehshua (Jesus) and His righteous Saints will neither judge after the sight of the eyes, nor reprove after the hearing of the ears; but rather, they will treat every being with dignity and with respect. Amen. We pray that YOU hasten the establishment of this kingdom so that all of humanity who have never known YOUR laws (or ways) will at last have access to that wonderful, saving knowledge because of the binding of Satan and the removal of his power (or influence) over the whole of humanity so that we are no longer deceived by him. Amen (Mat. 8:11; 12:28; Lk. 11:20; 13:28-29; Isa. 2:3-4; 11:4, 6-9; Rev. 11:15; 19:15-16).

We petition YOUR throne of grace to quickly establish this kingdom that will fill the earth with the true knowledge of both YOU and the Messiah (Christ), thereby causing that perfect and unparalleled peace that the world has never experienced to break out in our lives, families, communities and nations. Amen. We beseech YOU to establish this government in which all of humanity will be taught how to truly live instead of teaching us how to make a living and in which the principles for healthy and lasting relationships will be thoroughly explained so that all forms of interpersonal conflicts will be eradicated. Amen. We pray for the establishment of this kingdom in which harmony will be restored within YOUR creation causing the cessation of all manner of disputes and wars that have continued to plague mankind for ages, and the disappearance of the enmity between humanity and animals and within animals so that all of creation will dwell in peace. Amen. We desperately yearn for the enthronement of this kingdom in which all wild animals will become tamed and peacefully dwell with defenseless animals of prey; we eagerly look forward to the establishment of this kingdom in which no animal will feed on flesh anymore but all will feed only on vegetation; and we crave the advent of this kingdom in which all deadly animals will become harmless and in which little children will play with them without fear of hurt. Amen (Isa. 2:4; 11:4, 6-9; Rev. 11:15; 19:15-16).

We pray YOU to hasten the establishment of this glorious kingdom during which YOU will bring healing to the whole of creation so that all forms of pollution and ill-health will disappear forever. Amen. We crave the inauguration of this government during which YOU will bring healing to the atmosphere so that there will be an un-ending gorgeous weather everywhere with the disappearance of all forms of storms (floods, tornadoes, hurricanes, tsunamis) and weather extremes; we eagerly desire the establishment of this utopian kingdom during which YOU will bring stability to the earth's crust so that earth tremors, earthquakes and volcanic eruptions will cease to occur and the weather will be so delightful that the occurrence of scorching heat, bitter cold or suffocating humidity will be completely eradicated. Amen. We implore YOU to establish this kingdom in which YOUR blessings will bring healing to the lands such that all lands (including deserts, thirsty lands and parched ground) will be glad and rejoice with singing because they will be generously watered so that the earth will be covered with meadows of luxuriant vegetation and experience enormous explosion in the quality and quantity of food production. Amen. We yearn for the establishment of this utopian world during which perfect physical wellbeing and mental (including emotional) health will break out upon all of humanity due to YOUR healing of all our diseases and infirmities, the eradication of all deadly viruses and the disappearance of all lethal bacteria leading to cessation in the use of therapeutic drugs and the closure of all hospitals and clinics. Amen (Isa. 2:4; 11:4, 6-9; Rev. 11:15; 19:15-16).

We pray that YOU accelerate the inauguration of Yehshua's (Jesus') government during which all of humanity will dwell in absolute safety in our individual homes, enjoy the fruits of our labor, be completely satisfied with the enormous amounts of foods and drink that YOU will generously provide for us, experience equitable distribution of wealth and be exceedingly joyful because we will not lack anything. Amen. We pray for the arrival of this Messianic kingdom so that YOU can subsequently establish YOUR everlasting kingdom in which YOU will be King and Father of all, Yehshua (Jesus) will be the Prince and all others will be immortal members of YOUR divine family. Amen. We urge YOU to establish this latter kingdom in which YOU will personally dwell with us and wipe away every tear from our eyes; in which death shall be no more, neither shall there be anguish (sorrow and mourning), nor grief, nor pain any more, because the old conditions and the former order of things would have passed away; we beseech YOU to establish this kingdom, whose magnificence will defy any form of description and dwarf the limits of our imagination; we yearn for this eternal kingdom which is YOUR paradise that will be brought down to earth. Amen. Most awesome GOD, we pray that YOU continue to expound to our minds in vivid details the truth about the Good News of YOUR kingdom so that our hope in this coming kingdom is made perfect and help us to be found worthy to enter and inherit this kingdom. Amen. We thank YOU for giving us the honor to petition YOU for this kingdom, so that the Accuser does not claim that YOU are abusing YOUR power by unilaterally imposing YOUR will on us. Amen (Isa. 2:4; 11: 6-9; 35:

The Disciples' Prayer

1-7; 65:21-22; Dan. 2:44; Ezek. 11:19-20; 34:26-27; Micah 4:2-4; Amos 9:13-14; Rev. 20:1-3; 21).

GOD's Will: While we patiently await the establishment of YOUR glorious kingdom, we pray that YOU grant us the teachable spirit of children so that we may be well groomed in the internalization and manifestation of those attributes that are well-suited for kingdom life, thereby causing YOUR (perceptive) will to be done on earth as it is being done in heaven. Amen. YOUR will (desire) O good LORD is that everyone should believe in YOUR Word and be doers of it for the purpose of abundant fruitfulness in holiness (or holy living). Amen. YOUR divine will is that everyone should believe that YOU sent YOUR only begotten Son – Yehshua (Jesus), as the predestined and appointed deliverer from our sins, as the source of our righteousness and the restorer of YOUR subverted creation so that YOU may give us eternal life. Amen. And eternal life is that we may know YOU, the only true GOD, as YOU really are and to know Yehshua (Jesus) whom YOU have sent. Amen (Rom. 12:1-2; 1 Tim. 2:3-4; 1 Thes. 4:3-8; 2 Pet. 3:9; Joh. 6:40; 17:3; Mat. 1:21; 1 Cor. 1:30; Gen. 3:15).

YOUR kingdom though virtual at present, involves the active sowing of YOUR pure and unadulterated Word (that is of inestimable worth) in the fertile soil of the minds of potential kingdom subjects, and accompanied with empowerment by (the) holy spirit for the purpose of living according to YOUR will (YOUR revealed standards and principles) so as to duplicate the life of the Messiah (Christ) in us. Amen. We thank YOU for 'seeding' this virtual kingdom at Yehshua's (Jesus') first coming as a little flock, and pray that YOU continue to expand its membership (citizenship) until it fills the whole earth. Amen. In accordance with YOUR will, we pray YOU to continuously energize the dissemination of the true gospel by continuing to raise anointed teachers and

Evangelists for every cultural group inhabiting the earth, and to unstop the ears and tenderize the minds of Unbelievers so that they will receive this Good News whenever they hear or read about it and come to true repentance. Amen. Continue to nourish and strengthen all Church leaders so that they may be genuine earthly shepherds of YOUR true sheep, and protect them so that they are not repossessed by the Evil One. Amen (Mat. 13:3-8, 18-23, 44-45; Lk. 8:5-8, 11-15; Rom. 8:29; 14:14; 1 Cor. 4:20; Eph. 4:23; Mat. 4:23; 13:24-52; Lk. 12:32; 13:18-21; Rom. 10:14-15; 2 Pet. 3:9; Joh. 21:16-17).

We exceedingly extol YOU because YOU have not left us ignorant or hidden YOUR Word from us, but have graciously preserved it in the Bible. Amen. In conformity with YOUR divine desire for us, we pray that YOU may help us come to the perfect understanding and unshakeable conviction that YOU primarily authored the Bible through inspired Writers, to acknowledge that it is fundamentally the only inerrant instruction manual the world will ever know for our daily living and to begin or continue to treat it with the sacredness it deserves. Amen. Continue to lead us into the perfect understanding of YOUR Word as YOU intended it to be understood and empower us to apply it in our lives. Amen. We pray that YOU may continue to teach, rebuke, correct and train us in righteousness through the power of YOUR Word. Amen. Grant us the abiding attitude to always meditate on YOUR unadulterated Word; let us constantly dwell much upon its diligent observance; let it (i.e. YOUR Word) permeate and soak up the innermost recesses of our minds; and let the water of YOUR Word thoroughly cleanse and purify our minds from all forms of spiritual filthiness. Amen. In this world of darkness, let the light of YOUR Word continue to guide and order our steps in our walk with YOU along the sure paths of life that are clearly defined by YOUR law (or revealed will). Amen. We acknowledge that YOUR

Word is like a spiritual mirror that clearly reveals our true spiritual nature and convicts us that without Yehshua (Jesus) and (the) holy spirit, we are spiritually destitute and eternally damned. Amen. Let us internalize YOUR Word intellectually and emotionally, so that it may become the spirit that is the sole controlling force in our lives, and the dominant factor shaping our desires, intentions, actions, emotions and motivations. Amen (Jos. 1:8; Psa. 119:105; Pro. 6:23; Joh. 6:63; 15:3; 17:17; Rom. 3:20; 7:14; 2 Tim. 3:16; Heb. 4:12; Jas. 1:23-25; 1 Pet. 1:23).

We highly exalt YOUR holy name for equipping us with the much needed power to be doers of YOUR Word through the gift of (the) holy spirit (our spiritual engagement ring) and pray that Evangelists will continue to baptize Repentant Sinners into the true Christian Faith (i.e. into the belief of the Father, and of the Son and of the holy spirit); that Yehshua the Messiah (Jesus Christ) will continue to baptize new believers into (the) holy spirit; and that (the) holy spirit will continue to baptize (or wean) new converts into YOUR true Church [the body of Yehshua (Jesus)]. Amen. We urge YOU to empower us to conduct ourselves each day according to YOUR revealed ways and standards so that we may continue to abound in YOUR righteousness, peace and joy through (the) holy spirit. Amen. Help us to be immovably committed to the symbolism of the outward sign of our baptismal rites; grant us absolute conviction in our cleansing with the water of YOUR Word; grant us the firm certitude in the burial of our former sinful lifestyle (or old self) in the baptismal grave so that we should no longer be slaves to sin; and grant us a concrete assuredness in our resurrection from the baptismal grave with the power of a new spirit-filled life of YOUR divine nature. Amen (Mat. 3:11; Mk. 1:8; Lk. 3:16; Joh. 1:33; Acts 1:5; 11:16; 1 Cor. 12:13; Rom. 6:3-14; 7:5; 8:13; 14:17; 1 Cor. 4:20; Col. 3:5).

Help us to fully cooperate with the promptings of (the) holy spirit so that YOUR implanted Word in the fertile soil of our minds will continue to bear in us, in an ever-increasing measure, the multifaceted fruit of YOUR divine nature. Amen. In harmony with YOUR commandment, we ask for the visible manifestation of the <u>fruit and gift of love</u>; let the transforming power of (the) holy spirit empower us to fulfill YOUR love injunction that requires us to obey YOUR commandments; let it help us to love YOU above all things and with every fiber of our being and to love one another as Yehshua (Jesus) has loved us, so that all our deeds will be motivated by genuine love. Amen. We ask for empowerment so that we do not have any gods besides YOU as our one and only GOD; do not allow us to make unto ourselves any graven images or the likeness of anything in heaven above, upon the earth or beneath the earth with the intention to offer worship; do not allow us to treat YOUR name in a disrespectful or worthless manner; and always help us to keep YOUR Sabbath day holy (separate) as a sign of our acknowledgement that YOU are the sole creator of the universe. Amen. We beseech YOU for empowerment to always honor our parents and the elderly; do not allow us come close to bearing false witness against any one or to committing murder, theft or adultery; and do not allow us to covet anything (including the good name or reputation of others) that does not belong to us. Amen. Grant us the power to love our enemies, to do good to those who hate or persecute us, to bless those who curse us, to pray for those who accuse us falsely and to accept all forms of ill-treatment without the intent of retaliating. Amen (Gal. 5:22-23; Deu. 10:12-13; Lev. 19:18; Mat. 5:43-44; 22:35-40; Joh. 13:34; Rom. 13:8-10; 1 Cor. 13:1-13; Jas. 2:8-11; 1 Joh. 3:14-15; 4:7-8; 2 Joh. 1:6).

In agreement with YOUR instruction for us, we pray for the full manifestation of the <u>fruit of righteousness</u> so that we may

The Disciples' Prayer

become addicted to following the leading of (the) holy spirit for the purpose of living a life of chastity (abstaining from unlawful sexual relations), holiness and obedience. Amen. We petition YOU for the visible materialization of the <u>fruit of peace</u> so that we may be overwhelmed with that inner calmness (or tranquility) which results from our confidence in YOUR willingness, readiness and ableness to cater for our needs and to deliver us from all our troubles. Amen. We implore YOU for the visible presence of the <u>fruit of joy</u> so that we may have unending and genuine gladness based on YOUR unchanging promises, goodness and sovereignty, and on an abiding attitude of praise and thanksgiving regardless of our circumstances. Amen. We beseech YOU for the full manifestation of the <u>fruit of patience</u> so that we may be adept at bearing provocation, annoyance, betrayal, misfortune, pain or delay without irritation, complaint or loss of temper. Amen. We implore YOU for the visible presence of the <u>fruit of goodness</u>, so that we may actively work for the best interest of others and with the ability to exercise fairness to all, especially to those who are of the household of faith. Amen. We ask YOU for the materialization of the <u>fruit of kindness</u> so that we may have genuine and tender concern for others, thus enabling us to treat others as we would have them treat us and as the Messiah (Christ) treats all true Believers. Amen. We beseech YOUR throne of grace for the full manifestation of the <u>fruit of faithfulness</u> so that we may always demonstrate and exude trustworthiness and loyalty, even as the Messiah (Christ) did. Amen. We pray for the materialization of the <u>fruit of humility</u> (or meekness) so that we do not think or see ourselves as better than others, and always exercise a gentle attitude that is patiently submissive in every offense, while harboring no desire for revenge or retribution. Amen. We beseech YOU for the visible presence of the <u>fruit of self-control</u> (or discipline) so that we may have the will and power to restrain our fleshly passions and appetites even when they are lawful. Amen. We pray that we

The Disciples' Prayer

may possess these attributes in an ever-increasing measure so that we are not ineffective or unproductive in our knowledge of YOU and of our Lord, Yehshua the Messiah (Jesus Christ). Amen. Continue to remind us that as the light of the world and salt of the earth, we are legal representatives (ambassadors) of YOUR kingdom and of Yehshua (Jesus) on earth, with full legal authority and through YOUR legal mandate which is our faith in Him. Amen (Mat. 5:13-16; 2 Cor. 5:20; Phil. 2:3-4; 2 Pet. 1:5-11).

In unanimity with YOUR counsel for us, we zealously covet the <u>spiritual gifts</u> of love, faith, hope and prophecy. Amen. Without absolute confidence that YOU exist and reward those who earnestly seek YOU, it is impossible to please YOU. Amen. We therefore ask that YOU perfect YOUR <u>gift of faith</u> in our lives for the greater glory of YOUR name; we pray that YOU grant us absolute conviction beyond evidence or logical arguments that YOU exist and generously reward those who earnestly seek YOU, so that we may be found pleasing to YOU. Amen. We pray for the imputation (or transference) of the living faith that was in Yehshua (Jesus) and in our Apostolic Fathers into us, so that we may be empowered to do the works they did. Amen. Grant us an unshakable confidence in, and reliance on YOUR Word as absolutely true, and the belief that it can never mislead us; help us come to see that as the rain and the snow come down from heaven, and do not return to it without watering the earth and making it bud and flourish, so also the Word that goes out from YOUR mouth will not return to YOU empty, but will accomplish what YOU desire and achieve the purpose for which YOU sent it. Amen. Grant us absolute conviction that YOU deserve to be trusted without any doubts or reservations, that YOU love us like no other, that YOU best cater for all our needs and that YOU are faithful to all YOUR promises. Amen. Grant us that faith that will embolden us to unambiguously make known to YOU in prayers what we want; and grant us that faith that makes it impossible for us to doubt in our minds that YOU will grant anything we want, since whatever we ask for is YOUR will for us. Amen. Grant us that faith that will always make us sure to receive what we hope for and certain of what we do not yet see; grant us that faith that causes the cancellation of natural laws to produce inexplicable or miraculous results; grant us that faith that makes things that appear impossible to become possible; and grant us that faith that will always convict us of the unfailing assurance of YOUR faithfulness. Amen. Grant us absolute conviction that whatever we pray for in the name of Yehshua the Messiah (Jesus Christ) will be granted us, so that YOU may be glorified in YOUR only begotten Son; and grant us total and complete reliance on Yehshua the Messiah (Jesus Christ) so that streams of living water will continue to flow from within us. Amen. We petition YOUR throne of grace that YOU may continue to deepen, strengthen and concretize our trust (or confidence) in and absolute dependence on YOU and the Messiah (Christ) unto perfection. Amen (Isa. 55:10-11; Heb. 11:1, 6; Mat. 17:20; 21:21; Mk. 9:23; 11:22; Joh.14:13-14; 7:38).

Let YOUR <u>gift of hope</u> in the future restoration of creation be perfect; let the hope that was in Yehshua (Jesus) and in our Apostolic Fathers be in us so that we may become zealous in spreading the good news of the kingdom. Amen. We crave for YOUR <u>gift of prophecy and discernment</u> to be able to discriminate between diverse spirits and be empowered to strengthen, encourage and comfort one another and edify (or build-up) the church of believers. Amen. We are eagerly desirous of YOUR <u>gift of teaching</u> so that we may be anointed vessels for spreading the truth and power of the Good News. Amen. We deeply crave YOUR <u>gift of the word of knowledge and wisdom</u> so that we are empowered to accurately decipher YOUR Word and effectively deliver and apply it. Amen. We are profoundly covetous of YOUR

The Disciples' Prayer

<u>gifts of healing and miraculous powers</u> to be able to accomplish great things in the name of Yehshua the Messiah (Jesus Christ), for the greater glory of YOUR name. Amen. We yearn for YOUR <u>gift of speaking in diverse (or strange) tongues and its interpretation,</u> so that we may directly communicate with YOU, utter mysteries with our spirit, edify ourselves and experience spiritual refreshing and rest. Amen. We ask for a preponderance of these gifts so that we may be able to effectively worship YOU, hear from YOU and work for YOU. Amen (Mat. 7:33; Lk. 12: 31; 1 Cor. 14:1; 1 Cor.14:3-4; Isa.28:11-12; 1 Cor. 14:21-25; Lk. 10:19; Acts 1:8; Rom. 15:19; 1 Cor.12:8-11, 28-30; 13:1-3, 8-10, 13; Phil. 4:13).

We thank YOU for allowing YOUR Word which YOU have magnified above YOUR name to dwell in our minds. Amen. We highly esteem YOU because the indwelling of both YOUR Word and (the) holy spirit indicates that YOU and Yehshua (Jesus) dwell in us. Amen. We exalt YOUR most holy name for deeming us acceptable as habitable vessels for both YOU and YOUR only begotten Son. Amen. We therefore pray in line with YOUR desire for us that YOU completely transform the vessels of our bodies into perfectly fitting dwelling places; cleanse our minds of the enormous filth they house with YOUR Word which YOU have written in them; guard our senses (eyes, ears, skin and nose) so that they do not process information in such a manner as to lead us into sin; guard our mouths (or tongues) so that our utterances may be wholesome, comforting and up-building; direct our hands and feet so that they do not lend themselves unto unrighteous acts; and do not allow us to be mastered by things that are not beneficial to us or that are in disrepute before the general public. Amen. Completely transform us so that we may continue to deeply meditate on the things that are true concerning YOU, Yehshua (Jesus) and (the) holy spirit; let us always ponder on things worthy of sacred respect and adoration; let us continuously dwell profoundly on things that are in harmony with YOUR divine standard of holiness; overwhelm our minds with things that are morally clean and undefiled; occupy our minds with things that are amiable or pleasing in YOUR sight; and let us continue to consider reputable things that are generally acceptable in the world. Amen (Psa. 138:2; Col. 3:16; 1 Joh. 2:14; Joh. 14:21, 23; Jer. 31:31-34; Col. 3:1-2; Heb. 8:6; Phil. 4:8).

Teach us to increasingly discern and be completely submissive and ultra-responsive to the nudgings of (the) holy spirit, and increasingly make our minds impervious to the gratifications of our fallen human nature. Amen. We pray that through this communication conduit of (the) holy spirit, which is the seal that indwells all those who truly worship YOU in truth and in spirit, and which explores all things, even the depths of YOUR nature, YOU may continue to communicate (or reveal) YOUR thoughts to our finite minds. Amen. In this fallen world, we ask for empowerment to live like strangers and aliens who are longing for a better country that is yet to come, so that our conduct (or lifestyle) will make Unbelievers to glorify YOU. Amen. We are persuaded by an absolute persuasion that if YOU did not prevent YOUR only begotten Son from suffering a most shameful death to initiate our salvation, YOU will not withhold from us the manifestations of the fruit of the spirit nor the gifts of the spirit which we have humbly requested. Amen. We offer this prayer in the name of Yehshua the Messiah (Jesus Christ) who intercedes for us in the heavenly tabernacle, and urge YOU to grant all the requests made in this prayer for the greater glory of YOUR mighty name because they are in agreement with YOUR sacred Word. Amen (Mat. 5:13-14; 1 Cor. 2:9-10; 2 Cor. 5:20; Heb. 11:13-16; 1 Pet. 2:11-12; Phil. 1:6).

(Petition GOD for the manifestation of the most desired spiritual gift in your life and in the lives of those closest to you).

Give Us This Day Our Daily Bread

The LORD our provider (Yahweh-Yireh or Jehovah-Jireh), we affirm that as our heavenly Father, YOU are a most loving and caring GOD with inexhaustible resources to meet all the needs of all humanity. Amen. Into YOUR hands we commit our physical and emotional health needs; we depend on YOU to meet our feeding, clothing, housing, security, transportation and financial needs; and we also trust that YOU will bring healing to our web of interpersonal relationships within the family, body of believers, in our work place and in the public. Amen. Grant parents godly parenting skills; help spouses fulfill their roles as YOU originally ordained it in the marriage ordinance; grant singles (bachelors, spinsters, divorcees, widows, widowers etc.) the ever-sufficient grace to fulfill their calling; bless the labor of our hands with financial sufficiency; let children be godly, teachable (lovers of correction and discipline) and loving; grant all earthly rulers and those who are in authority, godly leadership and management skills; and grant all of mankind the spirit of godly neighborliness. Amen (Psa. 104:27-28; Pro. 3:11-12; 10:1; 17:25; 22:15; 23:15; Heb. 12:5-11; Gen. 3:16, 18-19; Eph. 5:23-25, 28: 1 Pet. 3:1-7; 1 Sam. 2:7; Pro. 30:8-9; 1 Tim. 2:1-2)

The Disciples' Prayer

(Make specific material requests concerning the most pressing material needs for you and for those closest to you).

In spite of what we have asked for and because YOU are all-knowing, we petition YOU to overwhelm us with those material needs that YOU know will be best for us, and pray that YOU bend our wills to genuinely appreciate them. Amen. Continue to remind us always that whatever we build in our strength is in vain, but whatever YOU build endures forever; that godliness (yearning for YOU) and contentment is true wealth; and that naked we came into this world, and naked we shall depart. Amen. When YOU do not meet a particular material need that we intensely desire, help us to consider that the granting of such requests may not be spiritually profitable for us. Amen. We stand on the promises of Yehshua the Messiah (Jesus Christ) that if we seek YOUR kingdom and YOUR righteousness, all our material needs will be met. Amen. We are convinced without an iota of doubt that we are diligently and zealously working towards attaining YOUR righteousness mindset, and pray YOU and Yehshua (Jesus) to overwhelm us with our material needs. Amen. In whatever way YOU choose to honor us materially, help us come to the realization that the objects of YOUR blessings (e.g. wealth, spouses, children, intelligence, etc.) are YOUR possessions, on loan to us; and we ask that YOU teach us not to use them for our self-gratification but to use them as YOU would want us to, for the greater glory of YOUR most holy name. Amen (Psa. 127:1-2; Job 1:21; Eccl. 5:15; 1 Tim. 6:6; Jas. 4:3; Mat. 6:33).

Forgive us our trespasses as we forgive those who offend us

O LORD our GOD, our ultimate healer (Yahweh-Ropheka or Jehovah-Ropheka) and the gracious Judge of the whole world, we come before YOUR throne of mercy to petition YOU for the forgiveness of our transgressions. Amen. When YOU created us, there was no sin in our nature because YOU created us innocent with respect to sin, but through our individual choices, we fell into sin. Amen. Most merciful and gracious Judge of the universe, we acknowledge that sin is the transgression of YOUR spiritual law and can be likened to the ultimate spiritual crime punishable by spiritual death; it is the arrogant rebellion against YOUR revealed Word and the partial or absolute unbelief in it; it is the conscious and voluntary rejection of YOUR holy will and the enthronement of either Satan's will or our self-centered will in our lives. Amen. We acknowledge that sin is spiritual wickedness, it is contrary to YOUR nature being the very opposite of YOUR awesome holiness; YOUR whole being reacts against it with divine repulsion, YOU cannot bear to look upon sin and YOU are compelled to turn away from it. Amen. Sin in thought, word or deed is an abomination to YOU; YOU hate all workers of iniquity and YOU are angry with the wicked everyday. Amen. Since sin is the very antithesis (direct opposite) of YOUR nature, the destroyer and enemy of YOUR creation and since YOUR nature demands that it receives its full punishment, it behooves YOU to either discourage its occurrence or nullify its destructive effects. Amen. Consequently, in YOUR perfect justice and righteousness, YOU decreed that the just penalty for sin would be (eternal) death and that without the sacrifice of a sinless substitutionary life (i.e. shedding of blood), the destructive effects of sin could not be nullified. Amen (Gen. 2:16-17; 3:1-8; Ezek. 18:4, 20; Heb. 9:22; Rom. 5:12; Psa. 5:4-6; 7:11; Rom. 1:18, 32; 1 Joh. 3:4).

GOD most gracious, when sin entered YOUR visible creation, YOUR blissful relationship with all of humanity was destroyed and the whole earth became engulfed in the deep darkness of the "curse" (the destructive effects of sin). Amen. We confess that sin dwells in our flesh (fallen nature) and it is akin to a pandemic spiritual infection that causes a terminal spiritual disease, ultimately culminating in spiritual death; that all our acts of presumed righteousness are like filthy rags in THY sight; that no human has the innate ability to direct himself or herself to conform to YOUR revealed standards; and that none of us is righteous in THY sight because none truly understands YOUR counsel nor seeks to do it, but all of us have gone astray and none does good. Amen. We confess that our natural minds are hostile to YOUR holy law and incapable of submitting to it; that our uncircumcised minds are so deceitful and so severely diseased that no human can cure it; and that our sins have caused us to be quarantined (enforced isolation) from YOU, with the result that when we pray, YOU do not hear us. Amen. In the magnificence of YOUR love for YOUR creation, and because YOU are both a compassionate Physician and Judge, YOU decided to heal us of our spiritual disease, as it was threatening the survival and continuity of YOUR creation in accordance with certain redemptive (or curative) principles that are consistent with YOUR nature; YOU decided to heal our diseased minds of its insidious ability to generate sin *ad libitum* and to absolve us from suffering the just consequences of sins already committed. Amen (Gen. 3:1-8; Lev. 17:11; Pro. 16:9; Isa. 59:1-2; 64:6-7; Jer. 10:23; 17:9; Rom. 3:10-12; 7:17-18; 8:6-8; Heb. 9:22).

Consequently, in YOUR infinite mercy, YOU devised a way (spiritual maneuver) by which YOUR justice to punish sin can be satisfied and yet YOUR boundless mercy to forgive it (sin) can be triumphant; YOU devised a spiritual therapeutic principle that will reverse the prognosis (predicted outcome of a disease) of our lethal disease and make us whole. Amen. Since all of humanity had become contaminated with sin, each person owed a debt of (eternal) death, but none could pay the debt and yet live again. Amen. In YOUR unparalleled graciousness, YOU accepted substitutionary animal sacrifices under the First (or Old) Covenant because animals being intuitive creatures were incapable of sinning, but such sacrifices did not have the power to truly pay for or remove sins and therefore served to foreshadow the perfect sacrifice that was to come. Amen. In the fullness of time however, YOU revealed YOUR magnificent master plan by not only identifying the only acceptable sacrifice that will deal with the sin problem, but YOU went a step further to provide the perfect victim for the perfect sacrifice, in the person of YOUR only begotten Son, Yehshua the Messiah (Jesus Christ). Amen (Mat. 1:21; Joh. 1:29; Heb. 10:3-4).

This Yehshua (Jesus), the sinless second Adam is eternally priceless to YOU in that He has such an intimate relationship with YOU that no other being can ever attain. Amen. YOU made YOUR only begotten Son like us in every way, and of the seed of Patriarchs Abraham and King David. Amen. Through sufferings, He learned obedience and was made perfect, being tempted in all things, yet without sin. Amen.

YOU confirmed YOUR approval of Him by the miracles, wonders and signs YOU performed through Him and YOU gave Him authority to expound YOUR Word as no man ever did because He was YOUR Word in the flesh. Amen. During the Passover Feast in the last year of His earthly life, YOU placed the sins of all humanity upon Him and YOU treated Him as if He actually committed every sin ever committed by every person who would ever believe in Him, though He was perfectly innocent of any sin. Amen. Though He was not infected with the sin disease, YOU took infected blood samples from us and injected into Him that He may suffer the full consequences of this sin infection. Amen. YOU unleashed upon Him whom YOU love so completely the fullness of YOUR wrath against sin which was displayed (or manifested) in the cruelest form of torture, so severe that He was disfigured beyond recognition; His appearance was so awful that people looked at Him in astonishment and some thought He was being punished for His own sins. Amen. On account of each one of us He offered up prayers to YOU with strong cries and tears for deliverance; He was despised, falsely accused of being an impostor and rejected by those for whom He suffered; He was mocked, mercilessly whipped, spat upon and treated like the scum of the earth; He was made a man of sorrows acquainted with much grief; and finally He died a most miserable death from extreme exhaustion with condemned criminals and like one accursed. Amen. When we consider that father Abraham almost murdered his son of promise (Isaac) to prove his love for YOU, we shudder. But YOU unbelievably outdid Abraham in the sense that YOU actually allowed the murder of YOUR only begotten Son to demonstrate YOUR love for YOUR enemies. Amen. Most awesome GOD, we find this amazingly shocking and pray that YOU should let the intense agony and shame suffered by Yehshua (Jesus) in our stead be indelibly etched in our minds, and let the account of this tragedy continue to be

The Disciples' Prayer

replayed in our minds so that it may be for us a deterrent to sin. Amen (1 Cor. 15:47; Heb. 1:2-9, 13; 2:9-10, 14, 16-18; 4:15; 5:7-9; Mat. 1:1; 7:29; Joh. 1:14; 3:34; 5:19, 30; 12:49; Acts 2:22; Psa. 22; Isa. 52:13-15; 53:2-4; Mat. 26:67; 27:30; Joh. 19:3; 2 Cor. 5:21; Gal. 1:3-4; Heb. 4:15; 5:7; 7:26; 9:22; 10:9-10; 1 Joh. 2:2).

Whenever we confess our sins to YOU and affirm our faith in this perfect sacrifice of atonement, Yehshua (Jesus) our heavenly High Priest who intercedes for us, applies the merits of His one-time sacrifice unto us for the purpose of turning aside YOUR justified anger and taking away those confessed sins from our account because He suffered the full measure of YOUR wrath against all confessed sins. Amen. It is as though when we satisfy the conditions to receive the merits of His sacrifice, YOU take an anti-sin serum sample from Him and inject into us, so that the course of spiritual disease is reversed and spiritual healing progresses until the disease is completely cured. Amen. We humbly admit that we have all sinned and we firmly believe that upon confessing our sins, YOU are just and faithful not only to forgive them but to also purify our conscience from all unrighteousness. Amen. We ask that YOU grant us forgiveness for past and present sins and for sins repeatedly committed in our thoughts, words or actions, in what we have done and in what we have failed to do in our day to day living; and petition YOUR throne of mercy to forgive the besetting and hidden (or secret) sins that constantly assail us. Amen (Rom. 3:23; Jas. 4:17; 1 Joh. 1:8-10).

(Confess specific sins; ask for forgiveness and the strength to turn away from them).

We are without excuse for committing these sins against YOUR holy nature, even though they arise from uncrucified areas of our flesh and we take full culpability for them.

Amen. We pray for a genuine and true spirit of repentance for these sins; we ask for empowerment to turn away from them henceforth and beseech YOU to make us hate sin even as YOU do. Amen (Dan. 4:27; Mk. 1:4; Lk. 3:8).

We eulogize YOUR most magnificent name for fully punishing our sins and forgiving them on the basis of Yehshua's (Jesus') shed blood and for acquitting us of YOUR righteous judgment of death on account of His substitutionary but most agonizing death. Amen. We highly esteem and revere Yehshua our Messiah (Jesus Christ) for the intense agony and the sufferings He had to endure in order to effect the forgiveness of our sins even while we were His enemies. Amen. We bless YOUR most glorious name because YOU did not abandon us to our waywardness, for with YOU is forgiveness, and because YOU are a most merciful GOD overflowing with compassion and graciousness, and abounding in loving-kindness. Amen. We idolize YOUR most loving name because YOU did not continue to accuse us of wrong-doing, or continue to harbor anger indefinitely. Amen. We treasure YOUR most wonderful name because YOU do not deal with us as our sins deserve, or repay us according to our iniquities; as far as the east is from the west, so far have YOU removed our sins from us, so that they can never be remembered anymore. Amen. We exceedingly praise YOU because according to the multitudes of YOUR tender mercies and loving kindness, YOU have blotted out our transgressions from before YOUR presence; as high as the heavens are above the earth, so great is YOUR love for us, and as a father has compassion on his children, so do YOU have compassion on us, for YOU know that we are earthy (made of the earth). Amen (Exo. 12:3-13; Isa. 53:1-12; Mat. 27:46; Joh. 1:29, 36; 1 Pet. 1:18-19; 2:22-24; Psa. 130:4, 103:8-14; Heb. 10:17).

We bless YOUR glorious name because YOUR gift of our firm faith in the sacrifice of Yehshua (Jesus) has released

The Disciples' Prayer

YOUR healing power for our diseased minds; it has enabled us to receive from YOU a circumcised and transformed mind in which YOUR law is written and it has purged our consciences from dead works unto divine service. Amen. We exalt YOUR mighty name because not withstanding the depth and magnitude of our spiritual filth, the blood of Yehshua the Messiah (Jesus Christ), acting like the most effective cleansing and rinsing agent, has perfectly cleansed and washed us of our sins (spiritual filth), so that we are now as clean as snow and as white as wool. Amen. We glorify and honor YOU for transferring our sins upon YOUR sinless Lamb and for crediting His righteousness unto us, so that we may be justified in THY sight. Amen. We adore Yehshua (Jesus) for redeeming us from the curse which was upon us, so that YOUR favor (or grace) now rests upon us, that we (Gentile Believers) may receive the blessings given to Abraham and the promise of (the) holy spirit. Amen. We thank Yehshua (Jesus) for removing our alienation from YOU and replacing it with our much needed reconciliation to YOU, so that YOU now hear and grant our prayers. Amen. We exalt YOU O mighty One for bringing us to the realization of our helplessness concerning sin and our unworthiness of YOUR benevolence, and pray that YOU may perfectize and make absolute our trust in the redemptive power of Yehshua's (Jesus') sacrifice, so that we may be true beneficiaries of this awesome redemptive package of forgiveness, justification, sanctification and reconciliation. Amen (Isa. 1:18; 53:5l; Heb. 9:14; 10:7-18; 1 Cor. 1:30; 2 Cor. 5:21; Gal. 1:4; 3:13-14; Col. 1:21-22; Psa. 51:1-12; 103:11-12; Rev. 1:5).

We implore YOU to tenderize our minds so that we may be willing, desirous and able to forgive from the innermost depths of our minds all offenses committed against us. Amen. Empower us to forgive these comparatively infinitesimal offenses, even as YOU have forgiven us our mountainous transgressions. Amen. We pray YOU to completely subdue and destroy our inclination to seek retaliation for any offenses committed against us, because our vengeance can never bring about the satisfaction that we so intensely desire and because vengeance is within YOUR sphere of jurisdiction, not ours. Amen (Mat. 5:38-39; 6:14-15; 18:23-35; Mk. 11:25-26; Rom. 12:19).

(Confess specific unforgiveness and ask for empowerment to let go of the hurt or offense).

Father most gracious, we also pray that YOU grant us godly sorrow, a contrite spirit and genuine humility to sincerely seek forgiveness from those whom we have offended. Amen.

(If pride or any other vice is holding you back from seeking forgiveness from others, specifically admit it and ask for empowerment to humble yourself).

We pray YOU to make perfect our confidence (or faith) in the efficacy of the substitutionary sacrifice of Yehshua (Jesus) and in the blood of the Lamb in making pardon for our sins and justification in THY eyes complete. On the basis of the recognition and intimate experience of the efficacy of this sacrifice, lead us to enter into the rest of enjoying the fullness of the merits of the Messiah's (Christ's) sacrifice and become partakers in YOUR divine nature. Amen. May YOUR graciousness (undeserved mercy) continue to glorify YOUR mighty name, forever and ever and may YOU endow us with YOUR forgiving spirit so that we may be as forgiving as YOU. Amen (2 Pet. 1:4).

We also petition YOUR throne of grace and ask for mercy concerning how we, the Gentiles, have treated YOUR Word with utter contempt and disrespect. Amen. As a result of Israel's rejection of and unbelief in the Messiah (Christ), YOU extended YOUR invitation to us as the wild olive branch to be engrafted into the natural olive plant of Israel and whose root is Yehshua (Jesus); we are the undeserving guests that were invited to the marriage feast of YOUR Son. Amen. Thus, even while we were without knowledge of YOU and steeped (or submerged) in idolatry and diverse immoralities, YOU had pre-ordained that we (Gentile Believers) would be part of Yehshua's (Jesus') flock, and would be called YOUR people, YOUR loved ones and sons of the living GOD. Amen. Yehshua (Jesus) commissioned the Apostle Saul (also known as Paul) as the bearer of YOUR Word to us and Cornelius the Centurion was the first gentile Christian convert. Amen. But as our number increased, the true gospel over time gradually became corrupted and was beautifully repackaged into a look-alike counterfeit gospel that has practically devoured the true gospel. Amen. We have gravely sinned against YOU O LORD; we have continued in our idolatry by creating and serving the gods of our imaginations; we interpret the gospel and YOUR Word through the lens of our idolatrous and immoral eyes thereby denying the power that comes from true godliness; Churchianity has supplanted the true Messianism (or Christianity) of the first century and we have replaced YOUR holy ordinances with human traditions; we have loved the world and the things in it (i.e. the world) above YOUR Word because we have continued to succumb to the lusts of the flesh, by indulging in activities that excite and inflame unholy sensual pleasures; we have continued to yield to the lusts of the eyes by allowing ourselves to be taken in by luxuriant living; and we have continued to bow to the pride of life by craving undue societal approval, honor and applause. Amen. By our conduct, we have brought great shame and dishonor to YOUR most holy name; we are not serving the purpose for which YOU brought YOUR Word to us, and we have caused an innumer-

The Disciples' Prayer

able number of prospective converts to become discouraged from truly serving YOU. Amen. In YOUR dealings with us, YOU have been most gracious and have always acted faithfully, but we have continued to do great evil in THY sight. Amen. We revere YOUR most holy name because YOU forewarned us to beware of the spirit of deception that will come against the true Church, but we have not heeded YOUR frantic warnings. Amen. We ask YOU for the forgiveness of these grievous sins and deeply desire a global revival that will re-establish YOUR true gospel of the kingdom so that the awesome power that usually accompanies YOUR true Word will re-appear on the face of the earth for the restoration of YOUR impeccable reputation and for the sake of YOUR most merciful name. Amen (Rom. 11:11-28; Mat. 22:8-10; Hos. 1:10; 2:23; Rom. 9:22-26; Acts 10:44-45; Mat. 24:4-5, 11-12; 1 Tim. 4:1-3; 2 Thes. 2:8-12; 1 Joh. 4:1; 2 Pet. 2:1-3; Jude 17-19).

Lead Us Not Into Temptation

O LORD our banner (Yahweh-Nissi or Jehovah-Nissi), the LORD of hosts (Yahweh-Sabaoth or Jehovah-Sabaoth) who scatters our enemies before our eyes, we humbly approach YOUR throne of grace and of ultimate power, asking YOU to prevent us from yielding to temptation. Amen. YOU are a GOD who is majestic in battles and we extol YOUR mighty name for revealing to us that YOU do not and cannot entice us to do evil, but that we are tempted by our lusts and by the Tempter (Satan). Amen. We acknowledge that Satan is our ultimate enemy and that in spite of the enormous honor YOU bestowed upon him, he was found guilty of cosmic treason, and since his exile from heaven, his work has been to thwart and oppose YOUR purpose and plans, especially as it affects our salvation. Amen. The Wicked One deceives and misleads all of mankind, having perfected the art of deception, craftiness and cunningness, especially because he counterfeits YOUR Word (teachings, doctrines and revelations) and causes doubt, unbelief and double-mindedness about YOUR revealed Word. Amen. In the Serpent all ungodly attributes find their ultimate and perfect fulfillment; he masquerades as the angel of light by working miracles and deluding his followers as to their eternal end; as the god of this world, he is the leader of all unrepentant sinners and backsliders, and the spirit at work in

The Disciples' Prayer

the sons of disobedience; he is the enemy of all that is good, YOUR accuser and that of all humanity. Amen (Gen.3: 1, 4-5; Dt. 13:13; Job 41:34; Isa.14: 12-14; Ezek.28: 11-17; Mat. 4:1-11; 10:25; 12:24; 13:25, 28, 39; Lk.10:19; Joh. 10:10, 12:31; Acts 13:10; Rom.14: 23; 2 Cor. 2:11; 4:4; 6:15; 11:3,14; Eph. 2:1-3; 6:11-12; 2 Th. 2: 8-12; 1 Tim. 5:14; Jas.1:21; 1 Joh. 5:18; 1 Pet. 5:8; Rev. 12:3-17; 13:2-11; 20:7-10).

We also acknowledge that we are not bullied into yielding to temptations, but of our own free will do we yield (or acquiesce) to the persuasiveness (or allurement) of gratifying the lusts in our flesh (fallen nature); and being the Master con artist, Satan advertises his end-product of sin in an appealingly deceptive outer package that we find irresistible. Amen. We are exceedingly comforted however, because YOU have mercifully made known to us that these temptations must surely come to us, but also gave us the firm assurance that none of them will be too heavy for us to bear, because YOU will always ensure that we are adequately prepared for triumph and because YOU always provide a way of escape for us. Amen. We know that of ourselves, we are no match for the least temptation because of the weakness in our flesh; for even when our spirit desires to do the right thing, our flesh yearns to do the opposite, so that our inner desire to do right is frustrated. Amen. But YOU are the GOD of hosts who fights our battles for us by empowering us both to will and to do according to YOUR good pleasure, and by providing us the necessary power through (the) holy spirit to help us effortlessly resist and overcome temptations. Amen (Mat. 4:3; Mk. 8:11; Jas. 1:13-15; 1 Pet. 5:9b; Mat. 18:7-9; Luke 17:1-2; 1 Cor. 10:13-14; 1 Thes. 3:3-4; Rom. 7:14-24; Phil. 2:13).

We urge YOU to always halt us from consciously thinking (or considering) of doing evil or that which is against our conscience. Amen. We beseech YOU to always

The Disciples' Prayer

halt our tendency of continuously savoring the contemplation of doing evil with strong imagination; and when our resolve begin to weaken, strengthen us so that we may remain faithful to YOUR Word and to the promptings of (the) holy spirit. Amen. We ask for YOUR pre-temptation protection by unmasking and exposing to us the schemes of the tempter, thereby arming us with the knowledge of his strategems even before he begins to execute them. Amen. We pray that YOU deaden our body members to the lusts of the flesh so that we are not enticed by and do not indulge in activities that excite and inflame unholy sensual pleasures. Amen. We pray that YOU mortify our sense of vision to the lusts of the eyes (or lusts of covetousness) so that we do not become overly delighted or taken in by riches or luxuriant living. Amen. We pray that YOU make us unresponsive to the pride of life so that we do not crave the grandeur and pomp of a vain-glorious life, including thirsting after societal approval, honor and applause. Amen. We beg of YOU to install a step-wise, negative mechanism increase in each progressive step of the temptation process so that the ultimate act of yielding is frustrated and confounded, thereby making us invincible and unconquerable in all manner of temptations, even as Yehshua (Jesus) was. Amen (1 Cor. 10:13-14; 1 Joh. 2:15; Mat. 4:1-11; Mk. 1:12-13; Lk. 4:1-8,13).

We thank YOU for revealing to us that during temptations we are engaged in active spiritual conflict against demonic hierarchies (rulers, principalities, authorities and powers) in this dark world and in the heavenly realms. Amen. We also applaud YOU for making known to us that this war which rages between our flesh (fallen nature) and our circumcised minds is not physical and therefore requires spiritual weapons of warfare. Amen. But we are confident that the ultimate outcome of this conflict will be in our favor because YOU have mercifully provided us with the necessary weaponry to prevail in this battle. Amen. As good soldiers of Yehshua the Messiah (Jesus Christ), we pray YOU to empower us to be combat ready at all times by adorning us with YOUR full armor so that we may be able to take our stand against the Devil's schemes and still remain standing after victory is won. Amen. Clad our waists with YOUR <u>belt of truth</u> thereby causing our minds to be continuously saturated with the absolute truth concerning all that pertains to our spiritual life so that we are not lured away by Satan's lies and deceitful schemes; let us be firmly anchored in YOUR truth so that we are not tossed about by every wind of doctrine or succumb to false or heretic teachings; and let this truth firmly hold in place all other armor for this conflict. Amen (Rom. 7:14-25; 2 Tim. 2:3; Eph. 4:14; 6:10-18; Joh. 8:31-32).

Clad our chests with YOUR <u>breastplate of righteousness</u> by making complete and perfect our acceptance of the imputation (or ascription) of the righteousness of Yehshua (Jesus) unto us, so that the seed of YOUR Word which is our source of spiritual life is not rendered impotent (or dormant) or within the reach of any weapon of the enemy. Amen. Clad our heads with YOUR <u>helmet of salvation</u> to keep us permanently assured of our eternal life, by protecting our minds from all the spiritually deadly attacks from the kingdom of darkness, so that our redemption which has been won by Yehshua (Jesus) remains intact and unassailable. Amen. Since it is impossible to please YOU without faith, make us adept in using YOUR <u>shield of faith</u> so that our unwavering and immovable trust in the admonitions and promises of YOUR revealed Word will be a formidable spiritual shield that will always extinguish all the flaming arrows from the kingdom of darkness. Amen. Clad our feet with the <u>shoes of the gospel of peace</u> so that we are dexterous (or skillful) at always proclaiming the good news of YOUR coming kingdom and the hope of a future blissful life in this kingdom. Amen (Psa. 37:12-15; Eph. 6:14; Eph. 6:17; Psa. 37:39-40;

Rom. 1:16; 1 Thes. 5:9; Heb. 9:28; Eph. 6:16; Heb. 11:6; 1 Joh. 5:4-5; Isa. 52:7; Rom. 10:15; Eph. 6:15).

Permanently place in our hands the double-edged <u>sword of the spirit</u> (YOUR Word) with which to vanquish all our spiritual enemies. Amen. Grant us proficiency in using YOUR Word to demolish strongly but erroneously held beliefs (strongholds); let YOUR Word destroy arguments and every pretension that set themselves up against the true knowledge of YOU; and let it take every ungodly thought captive and bring them into submission to Yehshua (Jesus). Amen. Let our minds be seized by the absolute conviction that YOUR unadulterated Word which has been magnified above YOUR name accomplishes all that YOU have decreed it to do and that it is the most powerful weapon in the spiritual world. Amen. Let our conscience be held captive by YOUR Word so that we will continue to demonstrate an unyielding resistance to Satan, thereby confounding him and causing him to flee from us. Amen. Continue to strengthen and increase us in the confidence that as long as YOUR Word continues to dwell in us, we have overcome the world because YOUR Word is greater than he (the Devil) who is in the world. Amen. Continue to increase our zeal in fastings, our fervor in prayers and our commitment to a lifestyle of always coming before YOU as our first and only confidant, with all manner of requests and in all types of situations. Amen. Keep on encouraging us to always pour out our hearts to YOU with the full assurance that true solutions to our problems come <u>only</u> from YOU, and no other. Amen. Finally, we pray that in times of weakness when we do not know what to pray for, continue to increase our confidence that (the) holy spirit will always intercede for us according to YOUR will. Amen (2 Cor. 10:4-5; Psa. 119:89; 138:2; Isa. 55:8-11; Mat. 24:35; Eph. 6:17; Joh. 16:233; 1 Joh. 2:13-14; 4:4; Rom. 8:26-27; Eph. 6:18)

(Specifically confess the temptations that you frequently yield to and ask Yehshua (Jesus) for the strength to overcome them).

We praise YOU because though the Devil's intention for tempting us is to lure us to choose death by enticing us to yield to our sinful desires, YOU however use such circumstances to test us for the purpose of determining if our obedience to YOU is truly genuine, and to build enduring character in us; YOU test us to see if we will continue to trust in YOU in good times as well as bad times (or in adverse circumstances), and to see if we will continue to persevere until YOU victoriously walk us through those circumstances. Amen. Let such testings continue to produce in us boundless joy because it is an indication that our loyalty and faith is attracting so much heavenly attention that we have been singled out for YOUR testing. Amen. We beseech YOU to continue to confirm our faith (trust) and perseverance unto perfection so that we may attain complete maturity, lacking in nothing. Amen. In our testings, lock us unto YOUR Word and help us to remain obedient; help us to quickly grasp the intended lesson YOU desire to inculcate in us and grant us the right attitude to accept such challenging circumstances until YOU completely effect the change that YOU desire to produce in us. Amen. While we await YOUR perfect will to be accomplished in all our testings, endow us with godly patience, equanimity, fortitude, endurance, and the unshakeable resoluteness of confidence in YOUR revealed Word. Amen (Deu. 8:2; 30:19; Phil. 2:13; Jas. 1:2-4; Heb. 12:4-11; Rev. 2:10).

If in the course of being tested, we reveal any weakness that requires to be addressed, help us to gladly accept YOUR loving and fatherly discipline as a means of correcting this breach in character. Amen. Do not allow us to despise YOUR discipline, for in this, we are convinced that we are

The Disciples' Prayer

being treated as true sons and daughters and not as illegitimate children (bastards); and though usually very painful in the short-term, YOUR discipline is always beneficial in the distant (or remote) future (long-term). Amen. Grant us the calm acceptance of our inevitable fate of meeting with disapprovals before men as a result of YOUR Word; help us to accept rejection and enmity when we experience them from our immediate family; help us to submit to the unbelieving world's hatred and persecution when we encounter them; and to acquiesce to diverse hardships when we are confronted by them. Amen. When we are afflicted by Satan or his demons on account of YOUR Word, empower us to joyfully and stubbornly bear these in accordance with YOUR holy will. Amen (Job 5:17; Pro. 3:11; Mat. 10:33-40; Joh. 15:18-20; Acts 14:22; Rom. 8:35-39; 2 Cor. 1:3-6; Col. 1:11-14; 2 Th. 1:4-5; Heb. 5:7-10; 10:33-37; 12:5-12; Jas. 1:3-5; 1 Pet. 4:12-13).

YOU O Lord are the only One who can make us victorious over those too strong for us in this spiritual conflict. Amen. We pray that our spiritual enemies who rise up against us be defeated before us; when they come at us from one direction, make them flee from us in seven different directions, because greater are YOU who is in us than he (Satan) who is in the world. Amen. Contend O Lord, with our spiritual enemies who contend with us, and war against them, for they war against us without cause. Amen. Since they seek our eternal life, may they be disgraced and put to shame; since they plot our ruin, let them be turned back in dismay; let them be like chaff before the wind and their path be dark and slippery, with YOUR angels in hot pursuit. Amen. Since they continue to hide their spiritual nets and continue to dig spiritual pits for us without cause, let ruin overtake them by surprise; let the nets they hide entangle them, and let them fall into the pits they dig, to their ruin. Amen (Psa.35: 1-8, 10; Deu.28:7; 1 Joh.4:4).

The Disciples' Prayer

Most powerful and gracious GOD, we exceedingly delight in YOU because YOU have mercifully put it in our minds that we should bestow our total and complete trust in YOU. Amen. Because we depend on YOU to protect us in this spiritual warfare of temptation, YOU will hide us in the shadow of YOUR indomitable might (or power) and YOU will be our refuge (shelter of aid, relief, protection, safety or escape from dangerous or adverse situations) and our fortress (fortified place of exceptional security or stronghold that cannot be overpowered); YOU will deliver us from the snare of the spiritual fowler (Satan) and from all forms of perilous (spiritual) pestilence, and we shall take refuge under YOUR impregnable wings of protection. Amen. Because YOU are our refuge and dwelling place, we shall not be afraid of the (spiritual) terror by night, nor the (spiritual) arrow that flies by the noonday, since no evil shall befall us, nor any (spiritual) plague come near our (spiritual) dwelling. Amen. Because we have made YOU our refuge and our dwelling place, YOU will give charge to YOUR angels (our spiritual helpers and coworkers) to ensure that we do not come to any (spiritual) harm; YOU will empower us to tread upon all our ferocious spiritual enemies and trample them underfoot. Amen. Because we know YOUR name, YOU will answer us when we call on YOU, YOU will deliver us from all our troubles and honor us with victory and YOU will let us behold the magnificence of YOUR salvation. Amen (Psa. 91:1-16).

Deliver Us From Evil

Deliverance Prayer: Most awesome GOD, our unfailing Deliverer, we confidently approach YOUR throne of infinite power and majesty to petition YOU for deliverance from the habitual expression (or manifestation) of any form of evil, irrespective of its source. Amen. We acknowledge that the ultimate author of evil is Satan, and that though all of humanity are born pure (or innocent) into the world, we quickly acquire the ubiquitous attributes of the ruler (Satan) of this kingdom of darkness, which subsequently become indelibly engrained (embedded, inscribed) in our minds. Amen. We also acknowledge that though YOU have given us a new mindset and all that is required to combat evil in any shape or form, as long as we live in our present tabernacle of the flesh, evil dwells in us. Amen. While we await the receipt of our glorious bodies that cannot be tainted even by a hint or speck of evil, we pray that YOU should continue to deliver us on a second-by-second basis from the natural tendency to express the works of the flesh which dwell in our minds; we pray that the gift of indwelling holy spirit will continue to inhibit at all times, the expression of any form of evil that dwell in us and cause them to become dormant and unfruitful. Amen (Mat. 16:16-19; 28:18; Mk. 6:7; Luke 10:17-19; Rom. 7:25; 8:5-8, 12; Gal. 5:17; Col. 1:11-14; 2:15).

The Disciples' Prayer

Most merciful GOD, we pray that YOU should make us unresponsive to the strong pulls that always lead us into gratifying the <u>lasciviousness</u> (feeling, causing and expressing lust) and <u>lust</u> (an intense, uncontrolled or illicit sexual desire or appetite) that indwell us, so that we may be delivered from the act of *fornication* (voluntary sexual intercourse involving unmarried persons) or *adultery* (voluntary sexual intercourse involving married persons outside their marriage); *sodomy* (the unnatural and abnormal homosexual relations between men), *lesbianism* (the unnatural and abnormal sexual relations between women) or *masturbation* (self-stimulation of the genitals for sexual gratification); *onanism* (or coitus interruptus; withdrawal of the penis in sexual intercourse so that ejaculation takes place outside the vagina), *incest* (voluntary sexual intercourse between closely related persons and forbidden by law or custom), or *bestiality* (unnatural and abnormal sexual relations between humans and animals). Amen. Help us to understand that YOU gave us a wholesome sexual desire (or appetite) for our delight, but also determined that it must be used within YOUR established guidelines for acceptable sexual practices, so that this phenomenal gift is not misused; let YOUR attribute of chastity (or sexual purity) that indwells our new nature completely frustrate our tendency to abuse this privilege. Amen (Lev. 18:6-23; Rom. 1:26-27; 1 Cor. 6:13, 18-20; Gal. 5:19; Eph. 4:17-19; 1 Pet. 2:11; 4:3-5; Jude 7).

Most awesome GOD we thank YOU exceedingly for creating us with an innate (inborn) theistic nature, but ask that YOU do not allow us to pervert the purpose of this wonderful gift into the practice of <u>idolatry</u>. Amen. We pray that YOU deliver us from the lure of idolatry (which is rooted in unbelief in an invisible GOD) by making unattractive to us the desire to engage in or encourage any form of *superstition* (system of beliefs or notions not based on reason or knowledge), *image worship* (divine honor paid to any created

The Disciples' Prayer

object), *nature worship* (worship of the sun, moon and stars as the supposed powers of nature), *fetishism* (worship of trees, rivers, hills, stones, etc.), *pantheism* (the acceptance of all gods due to the belief that since the universe is a manifestation of God, therefore God is in everything), *hero worship* (worship of deceased ancestors or heroes), *atheism* (or self worship) or the *worship of false gods* (e.g. wealth, career, spouse, country, etc.). Amen. Dispel our unbelief and ignorance by overwhelming our minds with the astounding revelation of the irrefutable reality of YOUR existence through creation and through YOUR Word; and help us to see that the purpose of our theistic nature is to develop an intimate relationship with YOU. Amen (Exo. 20:2-6, 23; 24:24; 34:17; Lev. 19:4; 26:1; Deu. 4:15-19; 5:8-10; 12:30; Act 17:16-17; 1 Cor. 10:14; Gal. 5:20).

We acknowledge that YOU are the source of true wisdom and all perfect knowledge and adore YOU exceedingly for creating us with an inquisitive nature and an innate desire to seek knowledge. Amen. We however pray that YOU deliver us from all shades of <u>magic</u> (the supposed art of influencing the course of events by the occult control of nature or of the spirits) and <u>divination</u> (practice of attempting to foretell future events or discover hidden knowledge by occult or supernatural means or by practicing augury [the observation and interpretation of omens]). Amen. We ask that YOU make unappealing to us our involvement in any form of *esotericism* (secret knowledge or doctrine intended for and understood by only a few initiates) and in the practices of *enchantments* (the art of charming by spell or incantation), *sorcery* (or *witchcraft*; the art, practices or spells of a person who is supposed to exercise supernatural powers through the aid of evil spirits or by harnessing occult forces) *spiritism* (or *spiritualism*; the practices or phenomena associated with the belief that the spirits of the dead can and do communicate with the living especially through those susceptible to their influence), and *necromancy* (the art of predicting future events by conjuring up the spirits of the dead). Amen. We praise YOU for revealing to us that YOU do not communicate knowledge or grant power through these sources and pray that we may never come under their influence. Amen. We beseech YOU to permit the incontestable superiority and the amazing simplicity of YOUR knowledge and power being manifested in us to shame and confound all those who are involved in such practices. Amen (Lev. 19:26; Deu. 18:9-14; 2 Kgs. 17:17; 2 Chr. 33:6; Isa. 47:12-15; Ezek. 13:20-23; Act 19:19; Gal. 5:20; Rev. 18:23; 22:8, 15).

GOD of all creation, YOU wonderfully made us to be capable of moderately expressing our feelings at both the conscious and subconscious levels through complex activities in the nervous system. Amen. We thank YOU for YOUR goodness in giving us food for bodily nourishment, wine to gladden our hearts and the ability to be merry (full of cheerfulness, joyous in disposition). Amen. We humbly ask however, that YOU deliver us from all forms of <u>incontinence</u> (intemperance; lack of moderation, due restraint or self-control in sensual appetites) and <u>debauchery</u> (excessive indulgence and intemperance in sensual pleasures) which is rooted in our natural inclination towards overstepping the boundaries of moderation in the enjoyment of sensual pleasures that YOU established for us in YOUR infinite wisdom. Amen. We pray YOU to deaden our body members to all forms of *loose conduct* (or *indiscipline*) including drunkenness (a habitual state of intoxication resulting from excessive consumption of alcoholic drink), gluttony (excessive indulgence in over-eating), revelry (unrestrained and noisy or boisterous merrymaking) and orgies (wild merrymaking; or a revel involving licentiousness especially in sexual activities, frenzied singing, dancing and drinking). Amen. Let YOUR attitude of <u>*self-control*</u> (or temperance or continence) that indwells our new nature completely frustrate our

The Disciples' Prayer

tendency to misuse these phenomenal gifts for the proper enjoyment of sensual pleasures. Amen (Exo. 32:6-7; Rom. 13:13; 1 Cor. 10:17; 2 Cor. 12:21; Gal. 5:19-21; Eph. 5:18; 1 Pet. 4:3).

We exalt YOUR most gracious name for adorning us with certain internal alarm systems which warn us of invading poisonous feelings that are unhealthy for our souls and which need to be promptly and properly processed so that they do not cause us irreparable (or permanent) harm. Amen. We eulogize YOUR most awesome name for creating us with the ability to recognize when we differ from others with respect to our opinions, beliefs or personalities. Amen. We confess that there is a natural inclination in us towards <u>intolerance</u> (unwillingness to recognize and respect differences in opinions, beliefs, preferences or personalities, etc.) because of an aversion to people who are different from us. Amen. We therefore ask that YOUR indwelling attitude of *tolerance* would continue to teach us how to respect and accept these interpersonal differences so that we may be delivered from causing or supporting *sects* (or *divisions*; groups of people united by especially religious beliefs or opinions that differ from those more generally acccepted) or *factions* (a group of discontented minority working together especially for subversive purposes). Amen. Let YOUR attitude of *tolerance* teach us how to express disagreements (differences in opinions) with mildness (moderate in type, degree, effect or force) and peaceableness (not argumentative or hostile) through meaningful dialogue (an exchange of ideas or opinions on a particular issue with a view to reaching an amicable agreement or settlement) so that we may be delivered from all forms of <u>contentiousness</u> (habitually engaged in avoidable quarrellings and in foolish arguments or disputings) including *disputings* (habitually engaged in debates, arguments and controversies), *dissensions* (angry quarrelling), *strife* (heated and violent dissension), and *feuds* (prolonged

The Disciples' Prayer

bitter quarrels). Amen (Pro. 13:10; 17:1, 14; 18:6; 20:3; 21:19; 22:10; 26:21; 27:15; 30:33; Rom. 1:29; 1 Cor. 1:11-13; 11:16; Gal. 5:20; Phil. 2:14; 1 Tim. 6:4; Tit. 3:9).

Most gracious Father, we pray that YOUR attitude of *tolerance* which indwells our new nature would continue to moderate our feelings of <u>dislike</u> for others so that we do not indulge in emotions such as *malice* (ill-will or desire to harm another), *spite* (bitter ill-will), *hatred* (intense or passionate dislike) and *enmity* (feeling of deep-seated ill-will, or engaged in unfriendly or hostile activities) or be involved in *murder* for whatever or any reason. Amen. Help us to understand, that just as lust is the seed for adultery, so also malice is the seed for murder; help us to appreciate that the manifestation of intolerance is an attempt to impose our ideas, opinions or beliefs upon others without due respect for their GOD-given freedom of choice. Amen. Indelibly inscribe in our minds that even YOU (the all-powerful and all-knowing creator of the universe) do not seek to undermine this freedom of choice, but YOU gently seek to convince us through genuine dialogue. Amen. Teach us to always present to YOU in prayers any differences that we find troubling, so that in YOUR perfect timing, YOU will help us properly process such disquiet. Amen (Exo. 20:13; Deu. 5:17; Pro. 10:12, 18; 15:17; Ezek. 35:5-9; Mat. 5:20-22; 19:17-18; Rom. 1:29; 13:9; 1 Cor. 5:8; 14:20; Gal. 5:20; Eph. 4:31; Col. 3:8; Tit. 3:3; Jas. 2:11; 1 Pet. 2:1; 1 Joh. 3:11-12).

We thank YOU for creating us with the drive of *ambition* for the purpose of achieving desired objectives through effort. Amen. We confess however that <u>self-ambition</u> (self-seeking and inordinate desire for achievement or distinction for the purpose of feeding one's ego) seems to dwell in us because of an overblown self-importance (pride). Amen. We therefore pray that YOUR attitude of humility which indwells our new nature would continue to rebuke the expression of this perverted drive so that we may be

The Disciples' Prayer

delivered from all forms of *jealousies* (mental or resentment at another's advantage over a rival), *envies* (unhappiness or pain at another's superiority, success or good fortune) and *rivalries* (an excessive egocentric desire to out-do other competitors). Amen. We thank YOU for creating us with the gift of <u>anger</u> which enables us to cope with challenges associated with perceived or actual threats to deeply cherished values or expectations. Amen. We know that anger naturally manifests itself when we perceive that we are wronged or suffer injustice, but we however confess that there is a natural tendency in us to pervert this emotion so that its expression with respect to intensity and duration is excessive. Amen. We therefore pray that YOUR attitude of temperance which indwells our new nature will constantly moderate the expression of justified anger in us, so that we are delivered from all types of *rage* (violent anger), *resentment* or *indignation* (deep and bitter anger) and *fury* (excessive rage that resembles insanity). Amen (Deu. 9:8, 19, 22; Job 5:2; Psa. 37:8; Prov. 14:29-30; 15:1, 18; 16:32; 19:11, 19; 23:17; 27:4; Eccl. 7:9; Mk. 3:5; Rom. 13:13; 1 Cor. 3:3; 2 Cor. 12:20; Gal. 5:20-21; Eph. 4:26; Col. 3:8; 1 Tim. 6:4; Tit. 3:3; Jas. 1:19-20; 3:16; 1 Pet. 2:1).

We thank YOU exceedingly for the gift of saving faith which is causing the gradual healing of our diseased minds by the power of YOUR Word, with the result that it is being replaced with a mind of flesh that is agreeable to YOUR Law. Amen. We thank YOU for sending Yehshua (Jesus) to rescue (or deliver) us from the vice-like grip of evil and to destroy the works of the Devil; we owe YOU a debt of gratitude because YOU have given us YOUR truth which empowers us to be set free from enslavement to evil. Amen. When we are found walking according to the works of the flesh or against the dictates of our conscience, we ask for a speedy spiritual rescue; grant us the faith to accept this awesome deliverance so that it may be appropriated into our lives; and cause us to be transformed from living a life of spiritual defeat to walking in the victory that has already been won for us by living like Yehshua (Jesus). Amen (Gen. 3:15; 6:5; Jer. 17:9; 31:31-34; Ezek. 36:26-27; Heb. 8:8-12; 1 Joh. 3:8; Mat. 1:21; 1 Joh. 2:13-14; 5:4-5).

[Specifically confess the vices (or works of the flesh) that are at work in you and ask Yehshua (Jesus) to deliver you from them].

<u>Authority Prayer:</u> O most wise GOD, we acknowledge that because of Yehshua's (Jesus') sinless life while He sojourned here on earth, YOU empowered Him to exercise absolute authority over Satan and his demon hordes, and through his sacrificial death on the cross, He completely disarmed all evil powers and authorities, made a public spectacle of them and triumphed over them once and for all times. Amen. Most awesome GOD, on account of His perfect obedience to YOU, YOU conferred upon Him, all power and authority in the earth, above the earth and below the earth. Amen. We highly exalt YOUR wondrous name because YOUR Word indicates that everyone who exercises faith in Yehshua (Jesus) by believing in His mission, His message, promises and instructions will also exercise this kind of authority over the kingdom of darkness through the indwelling power of (the) holy spirit. Amen (Mat. 16:16-19; 28:18; Mk. 6:7; Luke 10:17-19; Col. 1:11-14; 2:15).

In addition to being delivered from our formidable foe and from ourselves, we zealously ask YOU for self-evident authority over our flesh, fallen angels (demons) and the Devil as a living testimony of our complete and total deliverance. Amen. As we eagerly look forward to the ultimate and visible defeat of the Devil and his demon hordes, empower us to always overcome them by the blood of the Lamb and the word of our testimony. Amen. We eagerly desire to exer-

The Disciples' Prayer

cise the kind of authority that Yehshua (Jesus) exercised over evil spirits; we yearn for insight to recognize evil spirits; and we crave for them (evil spirits) to be subject to our authority over them and to obey the orders we give them. Amen. We intensely desire to exercise Yehshua's (Jesus') delegated authority to us through YOUR holy spirit so that we are empowered to go into enemy territory, bind demons and plunder their habitations. Amen. Help us to fulfill the ultimate purpose of our deliverance by duplicating the perfect life of Yehshua (Jesus) in us through the power of (the) holy spirit. Amen (Mat. 11:28; Rev. 12:7-8, 11, 17; 20:1-3, 10; Mat. 10:1; 12:28-29; Mk. 1:27; 6:7; Luke 4:36).

We pray YOU to grant us the power to overcome, so that we may be deemed worthy to eat of the tree of life, which is in YOUR paradise. Amen. Make us overcomers, so that we may not be hurt by the power of the second death. Amen. Endow us with the power to overcome, so that YOU may give us the hidden manna and the new name known only to those who receive it. Amen. Make us overcomers, so that we may receive authority over the nations and receive the morning star from YOUR hands. Amen. Grant us power to overcome, so that we will be dressed in white, and Yehshua (Jesus) will never blot out our names from the Book of Life, but will acknowledge our names before YOU and YOUR angels. Amen. Make us overcomers, so that Yehshua (Jesus) will make us a pillar in YOUR temple, and will write on us YOUR name, the name of YOUR city which is coming down out of heaven, and His new name. Amen. Endow us with power to overcome, so that Yehshua (Jesus) will give us the right to sit with Him on His throne, just as He overcame and sat down with YOU (His Father) on YOUR throne. Amen. We humbly make this prayer on the authority of the reconciliatory blood of Yehshua the Messiah (Jesus Christ), and with the assurance that He intercedes for us in the heavenly tabernacle; and urge YOU to grant all the requests made in this prayer because they are in agreement with YOUR sacred Word, and for the greater glory of YOUR mighty name. Amen (Rev.2:7, 11, 17, 26, 28; 3:5, 12, 21)

Conclusion

We stand on the promises of Yehshua (Jesus) our Lord and Savior, that anyone who asks receives, anyone who seeks finds, and to anyone who knocks it will be opened. Amen. We are further emboldened by His teaching that if we being evil know how to give good gifts to our children, we should be most assured with all certainty that YOU being infinitely good, will grant us gifts that are much more precious than our wildest imagination can ever conjure up. Amen. We thank YOU for accepting and granting all that we have asked for in this prayer, because we believe that our requests are consistent with who YOU are and in accordance with YOUR will for us and because it is being made in the mighty name of Yehshua (Jesus), for the greater glory of YOUR awesome name. Amen, Amen and Amen (2 Cor.1:18-20; Luke 11:9-13).

www.ingramcontent.com/pod-product-compliance
Ingram Content Group UK Ltd.
Pitfield, Milton Keynes, MK11 3LW, UK
UKHW041949230426
12048UKWH00008B/221